The Complete
Airbrush Book

The Complete

Leon Amiel Publisher, Inc., New York

Airbrush Book

by S. Ralph Maurello

Formerly

Head, Instructional Graphic Arts

State University of New York, Plattsburgh

Director, Airbrush Department

Germain School of Photography, New York

Author: Commercial Art Techniques

Paste-ups and Mechanicals

Acknowledgments

To Ray Crouch, my assistant, I am indebted for his constant help in the preparation of this book . . . To the Paasche Airbrush Manufacturing Co., for photographs of their equipment and the use of some airbrush illustrations . . . To the many artists, firms, studios, advertising agencies and publications credited elsewhere in this book, for their contributions towards higher standards in airbrush illustration and its more extensive application. I am very much indebted to Roy Jensen, Production Manager of Leon Amiel Publisher, for his personal efforts and guidance in making this new edition possible.

© 1980 by LEON AMIEL PUBLISHER, Inc.

ISBN 0-8148-0755-0

PRINTED AND MANUFACTURED IN THE UNITED STATES OF AMERICA

Published by
LEON AMIEL PUBLISHER, Inc.
31 West 46th Street
New York, New York 10036

Dedicated to My Sister
Mary

Table of Contents

Introduction

The airbrush is an instrument used to apply paint to a surface. The paint is placed in a color cup attached to the airbrush, and pressure for spraying is provided by a small air compressor or carbon dioxide tank. One of the most characteristic and important functions of the airbrush is its ability to apply color in soft, subtle tonal gradations which may range from the lightest discernible tint to complete opaque coverage. With the proper type of airbrush, any amount of control can be obtained, so that the paint can be applied in any pattern, ranging from a thin pencil line to a broad spray.

Airbrush is used in practically every phase of the commercial art field — in Illustration, such as figure, mechanical, advertising, architectural, and technical illustration; in Photo Retouching, both black and white and color; and in Design, such as textile, plastic, product, greeting card, and poster. The airbrush is also used as a tool for production air painting of toys, novelties, textiles, ceramics, display photographs, greeting cards and decorative paintings by means of stencils. Most production applications, however, are for factory rather than commercial art use and will be of little interest to the artist.

This book is concerned primarily with the equipment and techniques used in the application of the airbrush to art-work and photo retouching. Before any results can be achieved with the airbrush, control of the brush must be acquired, and techniques for obtaining desired effects must be learned. Anyone with comparatively good coordination of hand and eye can master the use of the airbrush. The application of that knowledge to design or illustrative work is a question of art training and ability. While some airbrush work may be rather shallow and lacking in strength, this is the fault of the artist rather than the medium, just as poor drawing or masterly drawing may result from the same pencil used by different artists. Given the requisites of coordination and artistic ability, however, it is still difficult to master the technique of the airbrush without any training or guidance. It is the purpose of this book to fill that gap. There are certain basic techniques which must be learned regardless of specialized application. Until the beginner masters these basic techniques, it is quite futile for him to attempt anything complicated or difficult, as such attempts will only lead to discouragement. On the other hand, a little patience and much practice, properly directed, will gradually result in complete control of a medium which can respond accurately to almost any demand made upon it.

This particular book on airbrush techniques was planned to incorporate the following features:

1: It is actually a complete home-study course in that it considers every phase of airbrush technique: the initial set-up of equipment, the operation of the brush, instruction in diverse working methods, and their application to all the various fields of airbrush art. The book was planned on the premise that the student has no access to personal instruction and that consequently the book must, in itself, be a complete source of instruction insofar as possible. All questions, problems and procedures are anticipated and considered.

2: The presentation of the instruction is as visually comprehensive as possible. All operations, techniques and procedures are broken down and illustrated step by step. Adequate space is allowed to present fully any particular subject. Since the size of the illustration is important in visualising detail, all illustrations, especially those of step-by-step procedures, have been made large enough to be completely understandable. A sufficient number and variety of illustrations have been provided to eliminate as much as possible the need for reading matter, though ample text is included. In line with this policy of clarifying the instruction matter and making it as simple as possible, text and corresponding illustrations have been placed on the same page, and, in most instances, the text is directly beneath the illustration. This eliminates the annoyance of having to refer to more than one page at a time in order to correlate text and illustration.

3: Since the applications of the airbrush in the art field are diverse and varied, this book treats each use separately so that specialized methods are adequately presented. In addition, any related instruction, such as the use of mechanical drawing instruments, the making of acetate masks, and many other working methods, is provided.

Fundamental working procedures and techniques are presented at the beginning of the book so that the artist who wishes to use the airbrush only as an incidental part of his art may do so. Such application is illustrated in the rendering of the Sno-Crop package design on Page 82. Here the function of the airbrush is limited to flashing the package in order to give it the appearance of a plastic material. The illustrator, John O'Hara Cosgrave, and the caricaturist, Sam Berman, for example, limit the use of the airbrush to minor applications, whereas Otis Shepard does his Wrigley ads almost entirely in airbrush. More extensive use of the airbrush is progressively indicated in this book to the point where, except for minor line work, the artwork is done completely with the airbrush, as in the architectural rendering on Page 126.

Since so many applications of the airbrush and their corresponding techniques are presented here, this book will be of value not only to the artist but to art directors, production men, photographers, and many others who, though not wanting to use the airbrush themselves, can profit from knowledge of its performance.

Introduction to the New Edition

Since the publication of this book in 1955, it has been constantly in print, with no changes or additions made, though the instructional information is as applicable today as it was twenty five years ago. This new edition is being published for several reasons: Some of the examples of airbrush art in the book were becoming obviously dated (a matter of style, however, not of airbrush technique); it was possible at this time to add 16 pages of full color, thus enhancing the visual understanding and impact of the artwork presented, Airbrush, especially in the past few years, has been applied with increasing popularity and significance to the execution of fine arts painting and printmaking (as distinguished from commercial art); the availability of acrylic paints, water soluble during use, but water proof after drying provides a medium for airbrush which is as durable as oil painting; and, for some reason or other the space age and airbrush seem to provide a compatible partnership. In addition, color printing has made many technological advances since 1955, making possible more accurate reproduction of the subtle tonalities as well as the versatile texture and color effects obtainable with the airbrush, as exemplified by the full color illustration on page 16a.

Because of the insertion of color pages at limited locations and the black and white pages having been previously determined and printed, the natural flow or progression of material has been somewhat disturbed. However, this is a small price to pay for these additional pages in full color.

Elizabethtown, New York
August, 1980

Applications of the Airbrush

Applications of the Airbrush

The airbrush is capable of applying any liquid which can be sprayed, such as transparent or opaque water colors, dyes, thin oil paints, acrylic paints, gum arabic, photo emulsion, etc. This can be done in fine detail or broad spray pattern; depending to a certain extent upon the model airbrush used. The "oscillating" airbrush shown below is slow acting, allowing for complete control of fine detailed work—but not useful for comparatively large background areas; whereas the pencil type airbrush also shown is capable of very fine work as well as larger backgrounds or areas. More operator skill is required for very fine work with the pencil type airbrush. Thus, applications for the airbrush are numerous and varied in scope. As related to artwork, the rendering or painting might be done completely with the airbrush or airbrush combined with pen and ink line, or handbrush techniques. The airbrushing might consist of an incidental aspect of the finished art as in the "Contra-Schmerz" ad on page 16b, or

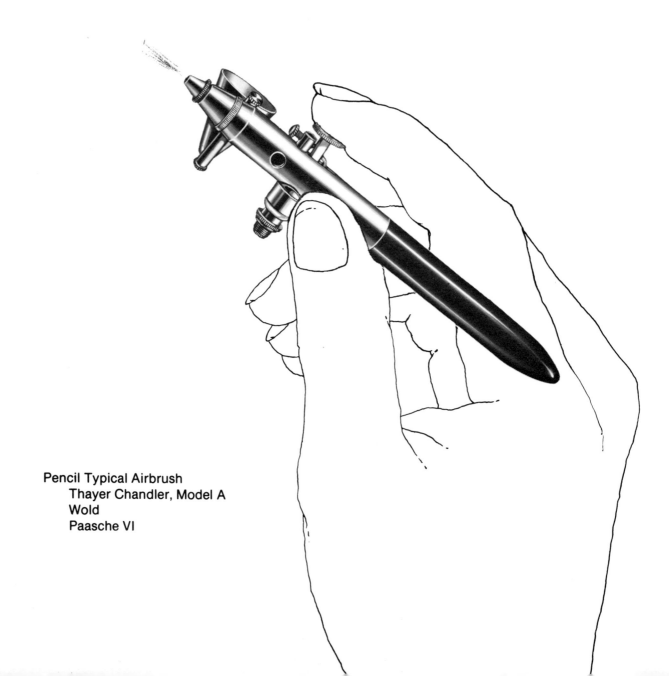

Pencil Typical Airbrush
    Thayer Chandler, Model A
    Wold
    Paasche VI

completely airbrushed as on page 16a. The contrast between the three-dimensional shaded pills and the flat pastor-like treatment of the rest of the artwork in the "Contra-Schmerz" ad is very effective.

Various broad categories of airbrush art include: Illustration, Design and Decoration, as well as fine arts painting and printmaking. Photo retouching is also considered an art application. Airbrush art is used for print reproduction (book, magazine, brochure, etc.); non-print reproduction (television, slides, film, etc.); and direct viewing (presentation, display).

Illustration encompasses many forms, such as Pictorial, Technical, Mechanical, Medical, Maps, Television Art, Visual Aids and others. On the next 8 pages examples will be reproduced of some of the art applications of the airbrush with a brief commentary in some instances.

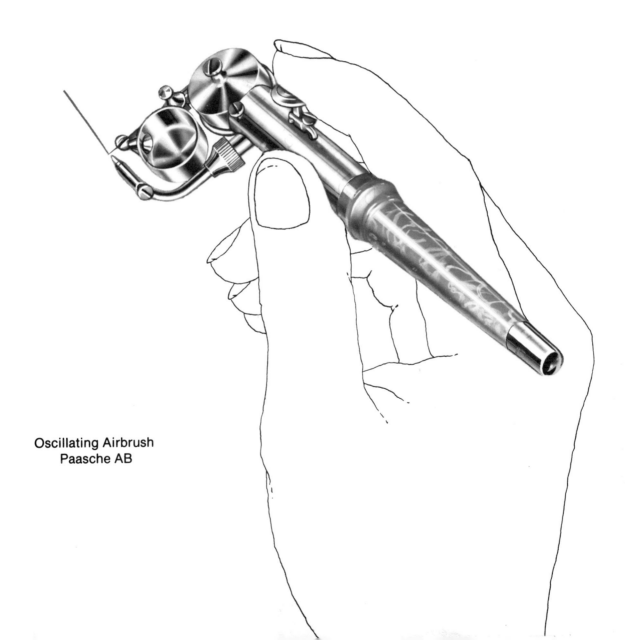

Oscillating Airbrush
Paasche AB

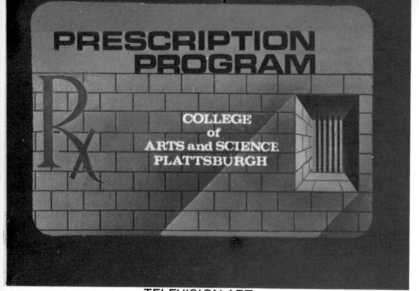

TELEVISION ART

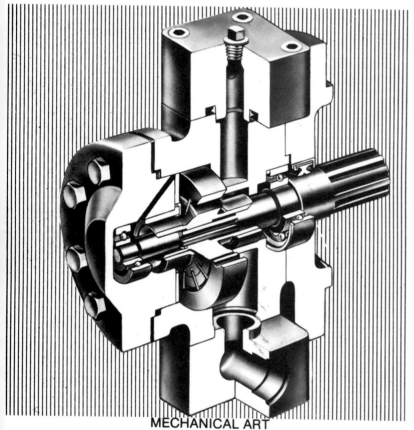

MECHANICAL ART

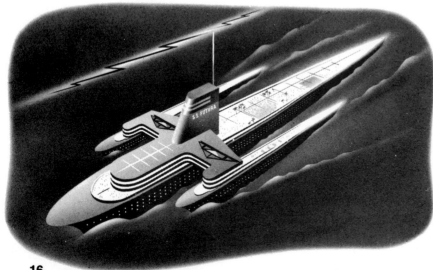

INDUSTRIAL ART

16

Product Rendering

Pictorial representations of newly designed products, from cameras to railroad cars, are made with the airbrush. Such renderings provide a three-dimensional picture of the product which is very helpful to the client, to the designer and to the manufacturer. The artist may work in conjunction with the designer and engineers when making such product renderings.

Technical Illustration

The airbrush is used extensively for textbook, manual, visual-aid and film-strip illustration of such specialized subjects as medicine, engineering, science, education, machinery, etc.

Display

Both the original design and the finished display can be airpainted. The design rendering of the display or exhibition unit serves as a guide to the client, to the builder, and to the artists painting the finished display. The larger airbrushes such as PAASCHE VL are used for this latter purpose.

Posters and Illustrations

General illustration, advertising illustration, and poster design can all be done effectively with the airbrush, the treatment ranging from extremely realistic handling, as in the figure illustration (page 16b), to complete stylization, as in the Pan American poster (page 16b). The use of handbrush line work to supplement the airbrush is usually advisable, to add strength and variety.

Design and Decoration

For flat print designs, such as greeting card, textile, plastic and paper wrapping, the airbrush is of value in rendering the original art, from which the design is printed mechanically. This is particularly applicable where graded halftone effects, and the effect of one color printed over another is desired.

Left: Joseph Binder, Roy S. Durstine, Inc., Seagram Distillers Corp.

Right: Illustration reprinted with permission of Hammermill Papers Group

In the future,
when you want your colors to burn with intensity...

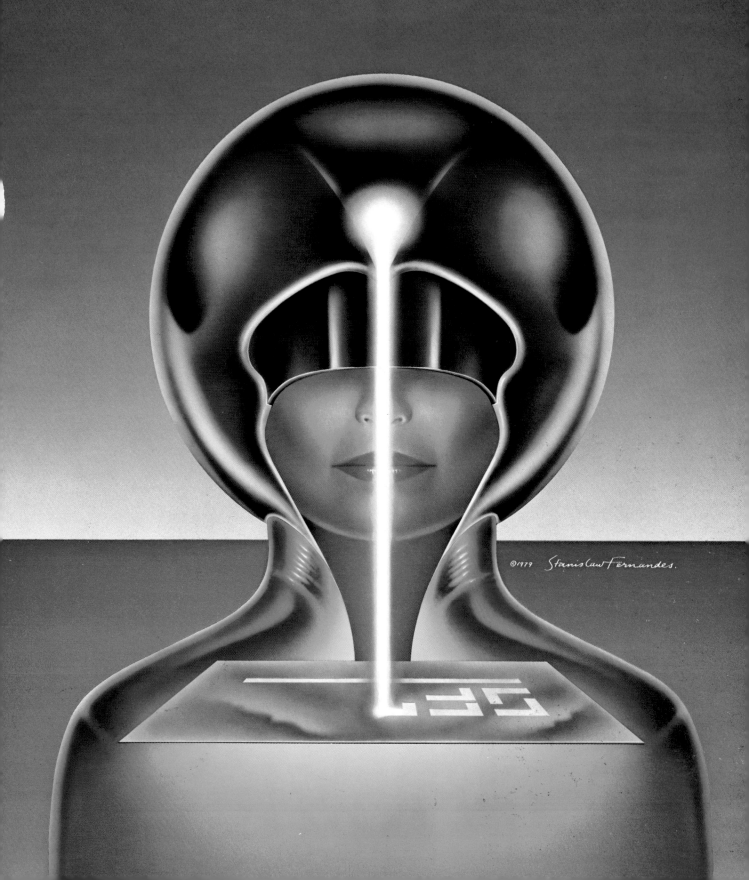

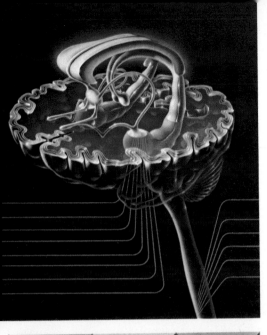

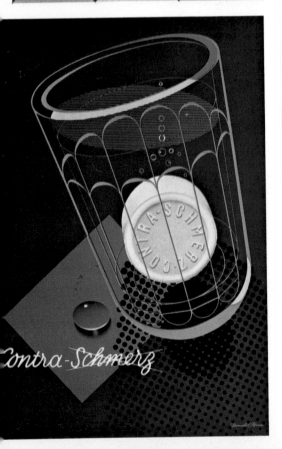

Contra-Schmerz

Tek
De Luxe
MEDIUM

Painting, William Wilson, Acrylic Airbrushed on canvas 58″ x 49″

Left: Product Illustration, Karl Koehn

Poster, Jean Carlu

NOW DIRECT SERVICE TO
SCANDINAVIA
by Clipper

PAN AMERICAN WORLD AIRWAYS

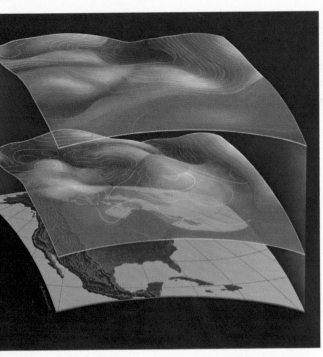

Left: Technical illustration. A. Petruccelli, Life Magazine
Right: Science illustration. A. Petruccelli, Life Magazine

Above: Mural design, Royaledge Paper Co.

Magazine illustration, A. Petruccelli, Life Magazine

Schematic, Mechanix Illustrated

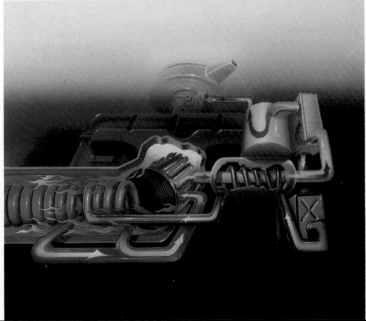

August 13, 1979 / $1.25

Newsweek

Can Chrysler Be Saved?

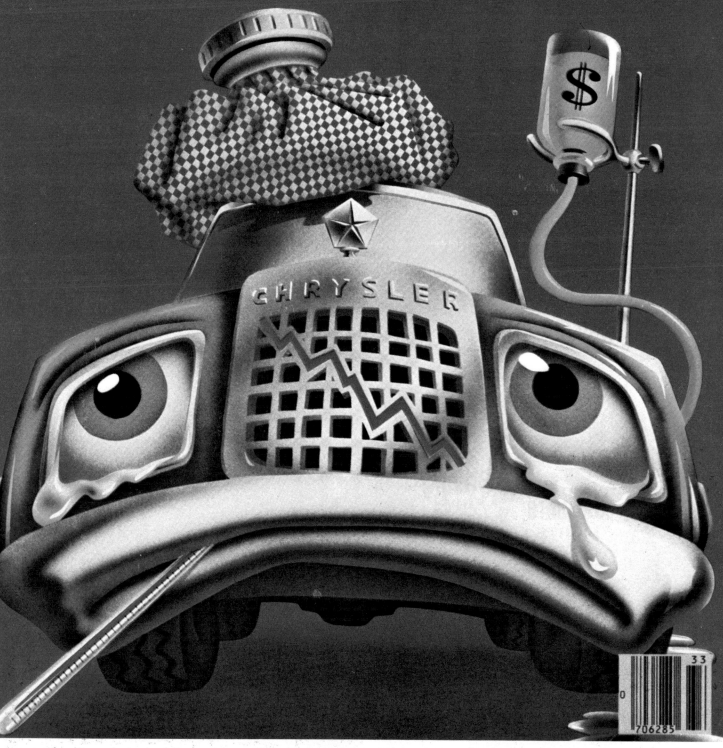

Photo Retouching

Photographs are retouched for several reasons, but primarily to secure better reproduction when printed in magazines, newspapers or advertising literature. Photographs may also be retouched to make alterations necessitated by the limitations of the camera or the photographer, the conditions under which the photograph was taken, or imperfections in the object photographed. Retouching may be done to affect structural changes in the object photographed, or to achieve a better appearance of the object. Photo retouching falls into various categories, depending upon the subject matter or the use to which the photograph will be put.

Editorial Retouching

The retouching of news, feature, or illustrative photographs for newspaper, magazine, or book reproduction is known as editorial retouching.

Mechanical Retouching

This involves working on photographs dealing with machinery or allied subjects, generally for catalog reproduction, instruction manuals or advertising uses.

General Advertising

General advertising retouching encompasses photos of all types of subjects from perfume bottles to automobiles, portraits, figures and pictorial material.

Fashion Retouching

As a general rule fashion retouching is considered a separate phase of retouching because of the specialized nature of the subject matter. While it does not involve the extensive knowledge and skill required of a mechanical retoucher, it has to be done carefully as material textures and naturalness of appearance are of considerable importance, as are the anatomy and skin texture of the model.

Portrait Restoration

The restoration of portrait photographs may also be considered a specialized phase of photo retouching because of the nature of the work and the subject matter. Faded or mutilated photographs are copied, then restored by airbrush retouching.

Original Photo

Retouched Photo, Ray Crouch

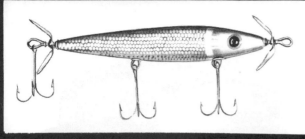

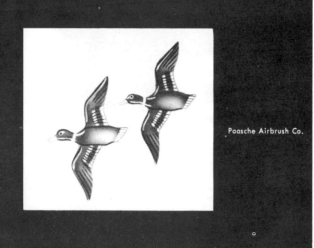

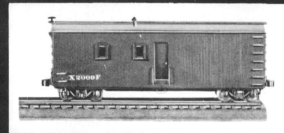

A MERRY CHRISTMAS

Airbrush Production

The duplication of artwork on paper, textiles or three-dimensional objects may be considered a production phase of airpainting . . . or "spraying," as it is known commercially. While the scope of this book is the application of the airbrush to original art rather than to the duplication of the same artwork, mention is made of this field because of the vocational opportunities it offers.

Plastics

Since it is expensive, and often impractical to manufacture plastic objects composed of many different or blending colors, dyes are sprayed on the objects with the airbrush, using stencils where necessary. Household items, sporting equipment such as fish lures, novelties and many other objects are colored in this manner.

Ceramics

Glazes are sprayed on pottery and dishware to duplicate the design, and to secure the blending effects produced by the airbrush. This also applies to metalware.

Toys

All types of toys, such as dolls, balloons, masks, model trains, etc., may be airpainted, using dyes or lacquers in the airbrush.

Textiles

Designs may be painted directly on textiles as a substitute for, or in conjunction with regular printing methods, as many subtle gradations of tone or blending of colors are otherwise prohibitive. Silkscreen is often used to print the linework, and the airbrush used for coloring. Ties, scarfs, blouses and other items of apparel are "hand painted" in this manner.

Greeting Cards

The duplication of greeting cards, aside from rendering the original design, may be completely or partially done by airbrush, working freehand and with stencils and masks. Watercolors or dyes are used.

Equipment and Materials

Airbrushes and Air Supply Units

Paasche AB: For extremely fine, detailed work, this brush offers maximum control and precision. Water colors, dyes, and thin oil colors can be used.

Paasche Model VI: An excellent all around studio ai brush suitable for artwork or photo retouching, for d tail or background art.

Paasche V, Jr.: The same as the VI, but with the color cup made as an integral part of the brush itself, for easy color change in small quantities.

Paasche VL: A larger model than the VI, capable fairly controlled work. Useful for posters, display, bacl grounds and spraying lacquers or watercolors.

Paasche H: For broader spraying effects, with water colors, dyes, lacquers, and oils. Used by signpainters, craftworkers, hobbyists, and ceramists.

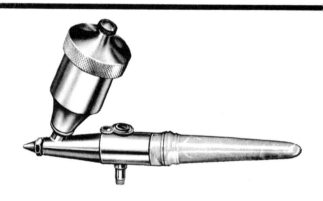

The Paasche Air Eraser sprays a fine abrasive inste of paint, and is used for erasing artwork, for cleani jewelry and dental appliances, etching on glass, e

Air Compressor, Automatic Operation: A diaphragm type air compressor, with air pressure switch and air tank base.

Carbon Dioxide Tank: A portable tank which holds ten pounds of carbon dioxide. This can be used instead of an air compressor.

Air Compressor—Continuous Actio Type: A compact, portable diaphragm type compressor, operating continu ously. Controlled by hand or foo switch.

The Airbrush

Several manufacturers make airbrushes of various types and models. The two basic types used by artists are the "single action" type and the "double action" type. In the single action airbrush, such as Paasche F and H, the paint flow is secured by one action — pressing down on the finger lever. These brushes are the simplest in design with the least number of parts. A color adjuster can be regulated for fine or coarse effects, but the spray pattern cannot be varied during a stroke, except by varying the distance from the paper. While good for background work and simple airbrush art, this does not permit the precise control that the double action airbrush does.

The spray pattern from the double action airbrush is controlled by two actions — pressing down on the finger lever and pulling back — the further back, the larger the pattern. This makes for easier control and variation of the pattern. The distance from the airbrush to the paper must be varied accordingly. The three major all-around studio brushes of this type are the Paasche V1 and V, Jr., the Thayer and Chandler Model A, and the Wold Model A1. These are capable of producing fine work or fairly broad work. A more specialized airbrush is the fine arts Paasche AB airbrush. This is used for the very finest detail work in photo retouching and air-painting, giving the artist absolute color control and enabling him to draw in freehand manner with pencil accuracy a wide range of patterns. It is a slower-acting brush than the VI, an asset in directing the pattern. The VL Paasche is a large double action brush capable of doing fairly fine work, covering large areas quickly, and giving a good heavy stipple or spatter when required. It is useful for poster, display and architectural rendering. It can be used for spraying lacquers or varnishes as well as water colors.

Sources of Air Supply

Carbon Dioxide: Pressure for the airbrush can be supplied in the form of *carbon dioxide,* obtainable in metal cylinders. This is the same carbon dioxide which makes the fizz for ice-cream sodas. It is obtainable in various size cylinders, the one containing 20 pounds of gas being the most practical. The full cylinder can be rented from a carbon dioxide dispenser or "carbonic gas" supplier. As a general rule, a deposit is paid on the cylinder and a monthly rental fee paid for its use. When empty, it is replaced by the company with a full one. To use the rented carbon dioxide cylinder it is necessary for the artist to purchase an air regulator to control the pressure of the carbon dioxide coming from the tank. (See page 156.) A complete portable unit with regulator, such as the one illustrated, can also be purchased by the artist. Carbon dioxide cylinders are noiseless in operation.

Air Compressors: A unit for compressing *air* can be used as an alternative to the carbon dioxide cylinder. This consists essentially of an air compressor and a motor to operate it. A compressor without a tank is a continuous operating compressor. It may either be of the diaphragm type or it may be of the piston type, which is sturdier and quieter. The continuous operating type is turned on by means of an electric switch, and will operate until turned off again. Excess air pressure escapes from a safety valve. Pressure can be regulated by means of a screw regulator or a standard air regulator with a gauge. The automatic air compressor has an air switch which is automatically turned on when the air in the tank falls below a certain pressure, and continues to operate until the pressure in the tank has been built up again. Such an air compressor can be located in a cellar or attic and the air line extended to the place where the airbrush is to be used.

Equipment

Most of the drawing equipment and supplies used by the airbrush artist are illustrated on these two pages. The need for and manner of using each

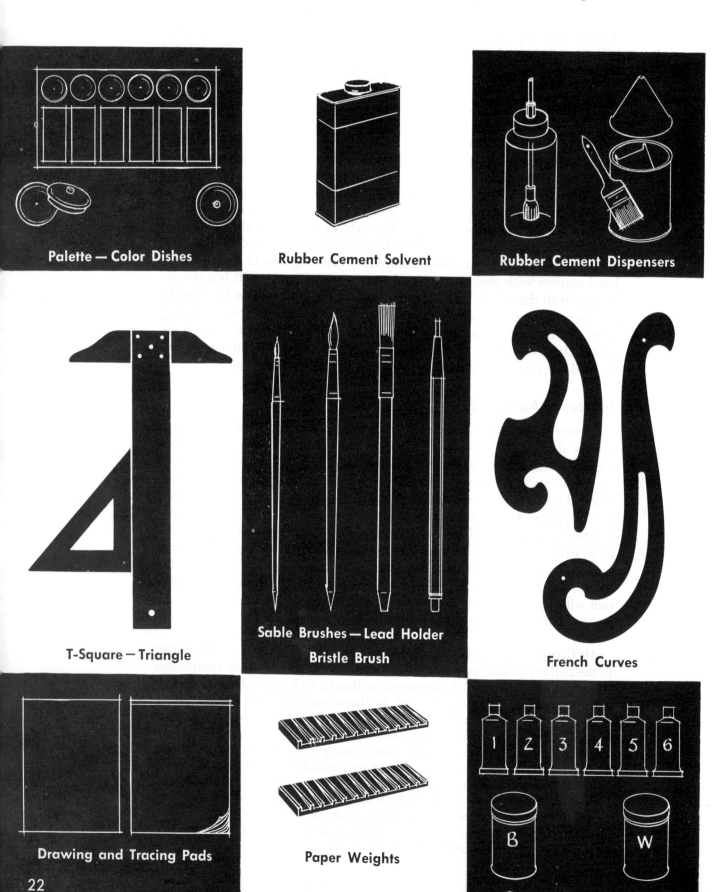

Palette — Color Dishes

Rubber Cement Solvent

Rubber Cement Dispensers

T-Square — Triangle

Sable Brushes — Lead Holder

Bristle Brush

French Curves

Drawing and Tracing Pads

Paper Weights

Opaque Retouch Colors

item is explained either on the next page or in its proper place in the book. Many of these items will be unnecessary for the individual artist unless he is doing highly specialized work demanding specific equipment.

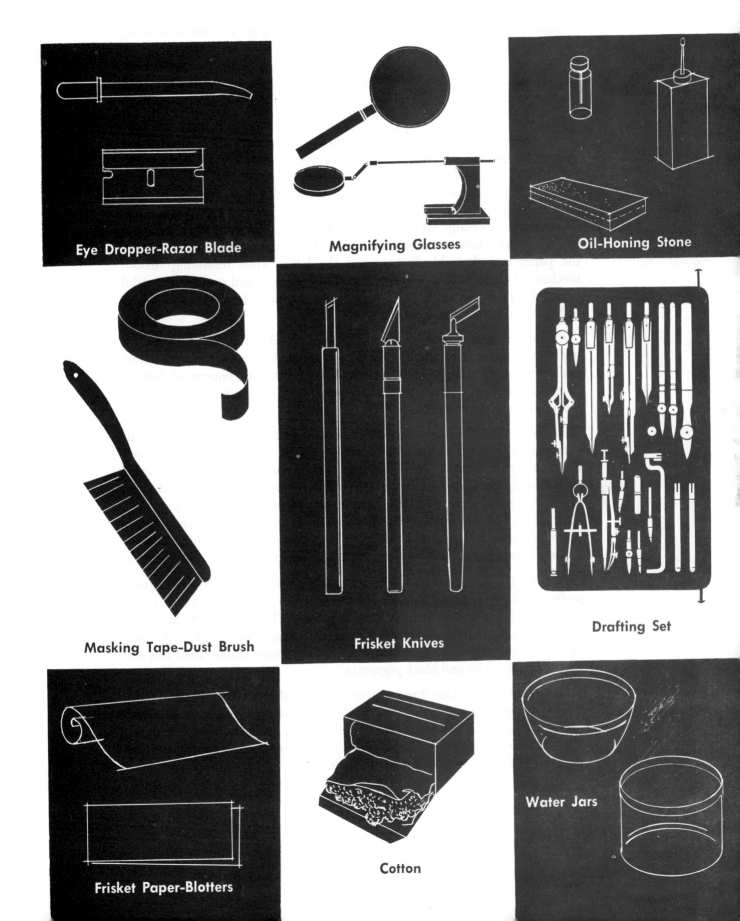

Eye Dropper-Razor Blade

Magnifying Glasses

Oil-Honing Stone

Masking Tape-Dust Brush

Frisket Knives

Drafting Set

Frisket Paper-Blotters

Cotton

Water Jars

Materials

Aside from the airbrush and source of air supply, the usual drawing materials and equipment employed by any commercial artist are used. The artist doing highly mechanical work will, naturally, require more specialized tools than a person doing textile design or fashion retouching. Basic materials and their uses are:

Paper: A good grade of paper or illustration board is required for airbrush, especially finished artwork. A thin, soft paper will buckle and the surface become marred when watercolor and friskets are applied. A kid-finish paper is best for general use, as a frisket does not adhere as well to very rough papers, and, conversely, a very smooth paper must be handled extremely carefully to prevent scratches or other marks from affecting the airpainting, especially when transparent color is used. Both rough and smooth papers, however, have their uses, the former when the texture of the paper is a desirable feature and the latter when rendering smooth mechanical surfaces. The Grumbacher Illustration Board and 3-ply Bristol Board are excellent for finished work. For practice, the 1-ply, Kid-Finish or heavy drawing paper is satisfactory.

Pigments: Our beginning efforts will be confined to the use of lampblack watercolor, used transparently. Opaque (Retouch) grays, tempera colors and dyes will then be used. More detailed information concerning these is given on Page 76. The airbrush manufacturers offer colors in these various forms, as do other art suppliers.

Brushes: Good brushes are very important as the handbrush is used in conjunction with the airbrush. Red sable pointed watercolor brushes, such as Grumbacher Graphic Arts, numbers 0, 1, 2, and 3, will be found most useful for general work. A larger one will be necessary where broad areas are to be painted in with the handbrush, as in newspaper retouching. (Throughout this book the term "handbrush" is employed to designate this usage, as compared with the "airbrush".) A round number 6 bristle brush is useful for mixing colors and cleaning out the color cup of the airbrush.

Palette: The flat plastic or porcelain palettes with round and rectangular wells, as illustrated, are practical, especially for retouch grays or other colors which are arranged in orderly sequence. The round wells are filled with the colors, and the corresponding rectangular slants used to thin out or "work" the color on the brush. The circular color dishes with lids are useful for the white and black pigments.

Other Items: Masking tape is used to hold the drawing paper to the board, avoiding thumbtack holes. Metal weights are used to hold down paper masks. A magnifying glass is helpful when using the pencil or handbrush for very fine, detailed work. The eyedropper is handy for transferring pigment and water to palette and airbrush.

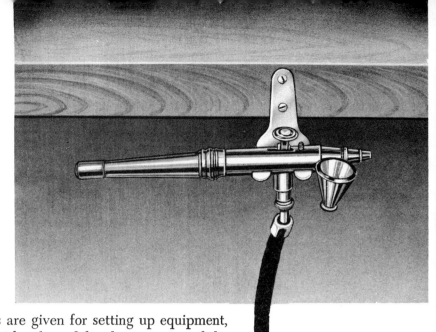

Basic Techniques

In this section detailed instructions are given for setting up equipment, for the care and maintenance of the airbrush, and for the operation of the airbrush.

It is advisable for all beginners to practice these exercises diligently as they are fundamental techniques which will be used regardless of the ultimate application of the airbrush.

Instructions for using the carbon dioxide cylinder and air regulator are given in the last section of the book. If you can take things apart but cannot put them together, merely read the instructions on airbrush repair, pages 150-151, but do not take the airbrush apart unless a more mechanically inclined person can assist you the first time. Actually, the Paasche VI, V,Jr. and VL are comparatively simple brushes to maintain in good working condition, which is one reason for recommending them to beginners. Any complicated repairs can be provided either by the airbrush manufacturers or by art supply stores handling the brushes. It is advisable, however, to be able to clean your airbrush, determine the causes of breakdown, and make minor replacements and adjustments. Properly used and cared for, an airbrush will last a lifetime.

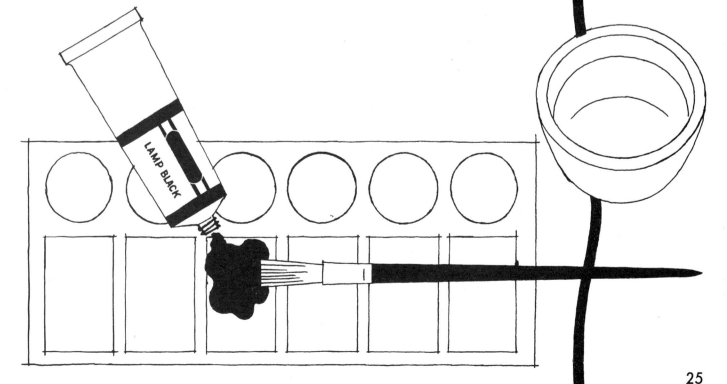

A Working Setup For Airpainting

A practical working setup for airpainting is much the same as that used by any commercial artist except that an air supply source is required. This is obtained either by the use of a carbon dioxide tank, as illustrated, or by means of an air compressor. It is necessary to have adequate lighting, as shadows from the hand and airbrush on the artwork are very disturbing, especially since the hand is always in motion when airpainting. An ideal set-up consists of a daylight source, preferably from the left of the artist, and a two-bulb fluorescent "floating arm" lamp. This lamp gives a soft light and is readily shifted to any position without the adjustment of screws or clamps. The airbrush, when not in use, is suspended on a holder. This should be on the right-hand side of the user to prevent dragging the hose across the lap while the airbrush is in use. (If you are left-handed, put the holder on your left. Airbrushes with the color cup on the left side can be obtained for the convenience of left-handed artists.) The taboret and other utensils should also be to the right of the artist. If the tank or compressor is objectionable at close quarters, it is possible to have it in some other part of the room, or even outside of the room, provided a shut-off valve is within easy access. The compressor can be put in a closet or in a felt-insulated box for soundproof operation. Several holes for ventilation should be drilled in such a box.

A single pedestal, adjustable-type drawing table is easy and comfortable to work on. Most illustrative airbrush work is done at a board tilted to about a thirty degree angle. Be sure the board is low enough to be comfortable, and avoid the tendency of many beginners to work standing up, as it is a habit which is not easily broken once formed. (It may be necessary, however, to have certain types of large work, such as display, in a vertical position, in which case it is practical to work standing up.) Do not keep your chair so close to the board as to cramp the action of your arms, for it is necessary to be relaxed and free from too much restriction when using the airbrush.

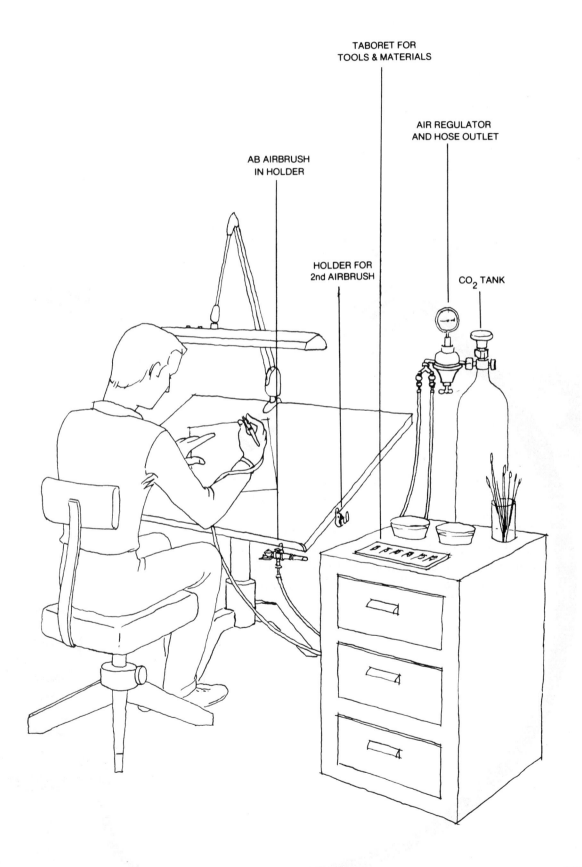

TABORET FOR
TOOLS & MATERIALS

AIR REGULATOR
AND HOSE OUTLET

AB AIRBRUSH
IN HOLDER

HOLDER FOR
2nd AIRBRUSH

CO_2 TANK

Getting Ready to Airpaint

Attaching hose coupling: If the hose is purchased without couplings attached, use those that are supplied with the airbrush. Slide the nut (top of the opposite page) over the end of the hose, then screw the coupling into the hose, as shown. The airbrush may be attached to the coupling first to acquire leverage for screwing it into the hose. When the coupling is in past the threads, screw the nut back up the hose.

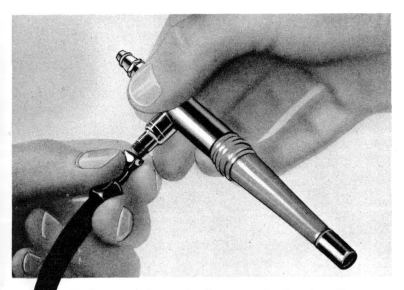

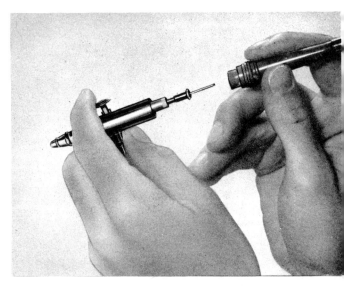

Before attaching the hose to the brush, allow some air to blow out any foreign matter. Screw the airbrush gently into the coupling, being careful not to strip any threads. As a general rule, hand tightening is sufficient, but if air should leak out at the hose connection, tighten the swivel nut by means of the small wrench which accompanies the brush.

It is advisable, before using the brush, to remove the handle and see that the needle is seated properly and tightened securely in place. Here, the handle is unscrewed, exposing the rear end of the needle.

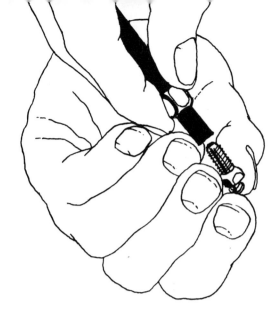

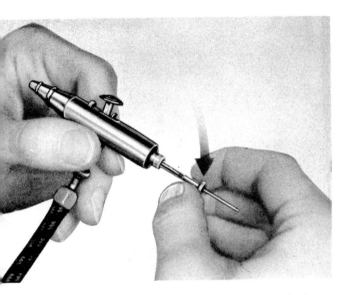

Turn the needle locknut (arrow) counter-clockwise to loosen it.

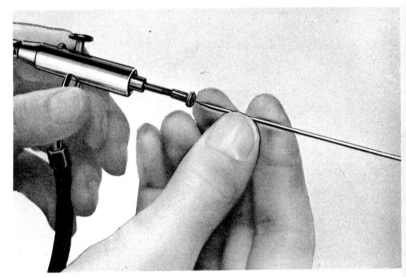

Gently remove the needle from the brush. You will note that the point has a very fine taper. It is important to protect this at all times and to handle it carefully as the slightest injury to the tip of the needle will result in improper functioning of the brush. When replacing the needle it is advisable to rest one of the fingers at the end of the needle locknut to steady the hand while the needle is being inserted.

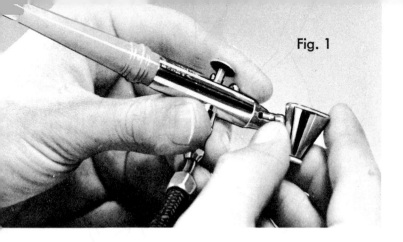

Fig. 1

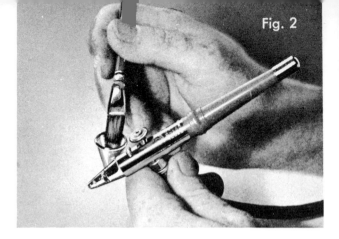

Fig. 2

FIG. 1. The color cup is attached to the airbrush by inserting it in the hole on the right side of the brush, forward of the finger lever. Do not force the cup in too hard or the hole will be enlarged. The cup is held in by friction; there are no screw threads. The cup should be adjusted so that it is in a vertical position when the brush is held at an angle of at least 45 degrees to the drawing board. [FIG. 2] Lamp black pigment is removed from the paint jar with a bristle brush and diluted with water *in the palette* to a fluid consistency, then transferred to the cup by means of a bristle brush or eye dropper.

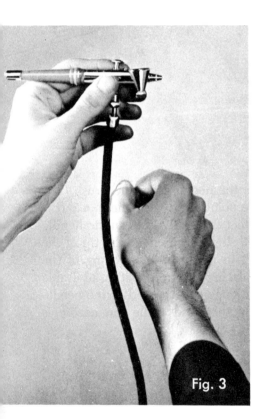

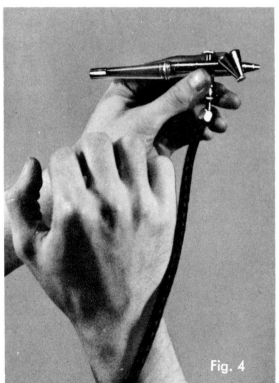

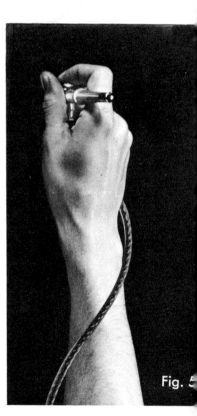

Fig. 3

Fig. 4

Fig. 5

FIG. 3. Hold the brush in the left hand and [FIG. 4] wrap the hose around the wrist of the right hand. Now, when the brush is grasped with the right hand [FIG. 5] the hose will be restrained by the wrist and not flop annoyingly over the paper or in front of the operator.

Airpainting

The manner in which the airbrush is operated is very important; therefore, these beginning instructions should be adhered to carefully. The operation of a Paasche VI airbrush is illustrated. The same procedure would apply for any "double-action airbrush." We will restrict our beginning efforts to obtaining a broad spray pattern. Sitting upright but comfortably relaxed and far enough away from the drawing board so that the arm can move freely, hold the brush about 8 inches above the paper and at right angles to the paper. Keep it at this height and perpendicular to the paper through the entire operation. Three distinct motions must be controlled and coordinated when airpainting properly. First, the hand is *set in motion;* secondly, the finger lever is pressed down releasing air but not paint; *thirdly*, the finger lever is gently pulled *back*, releasing the paint. The hand remains in motion during these three operations and continues so through the end of the stroke, when the finger lever is allowed to move forward, stopping the paint; then up, stopping the air flow; and, finally, the hand movement is stopped. It is very important that the three actions be separate, but follow closely upon each other. Running the first and second actions together will result in a sudden burst of paint at the beginning of the stroke. The movement should be comparatively slow and steady. Do not dip the hand or turn the wrist, or change the angle of the brush. The whole arm moves across the paper from the shoulder.

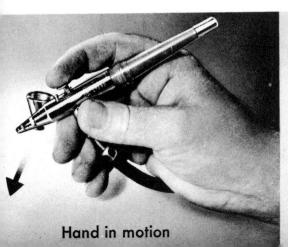

Hand in motion

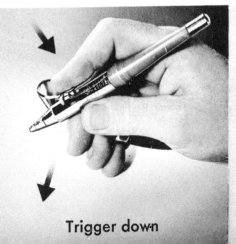

Trigger down

Trigger back

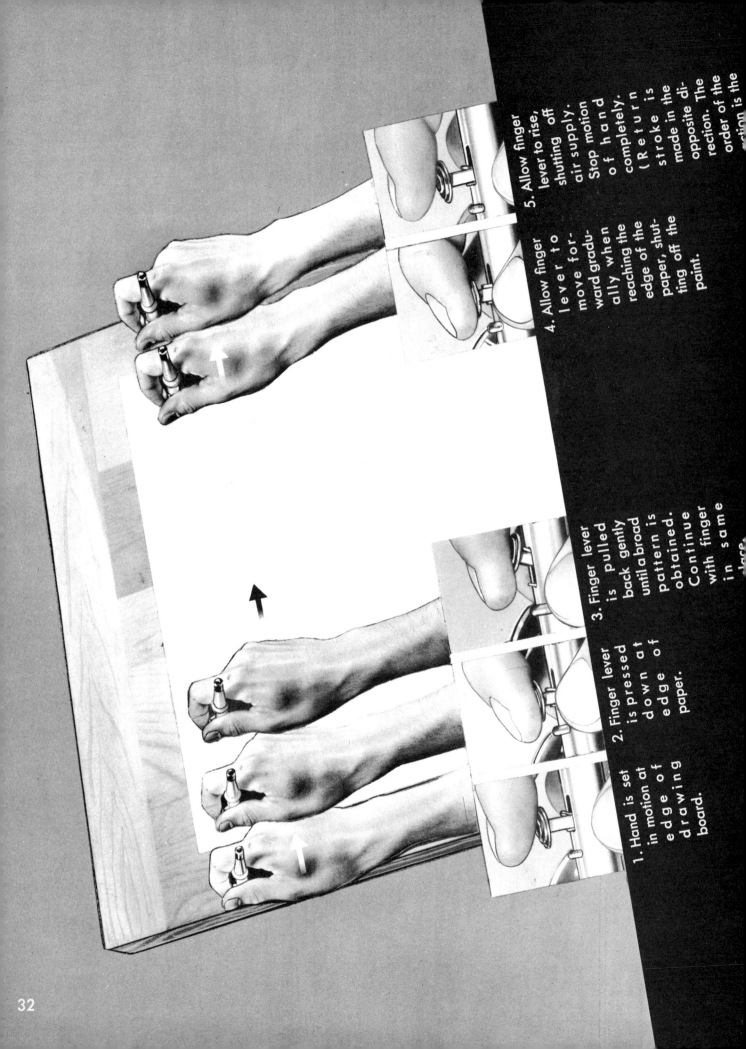

1. Hand is set in motion at edge of drawing board.

2. Finger lever is pressed down at edge of edge of paper.

3. Finger lever is pulled back gently until a broad pattern is obtained. Continue with finger in same

4. Allow finger lever to move forward gradually when reaching the edge of the paper, shutting off the paint.

5. Allow finger lever to rise, shutting off air supply. Stop motion of hand completely. (Return stroke is made in the opposite direction. The rection. The order of the

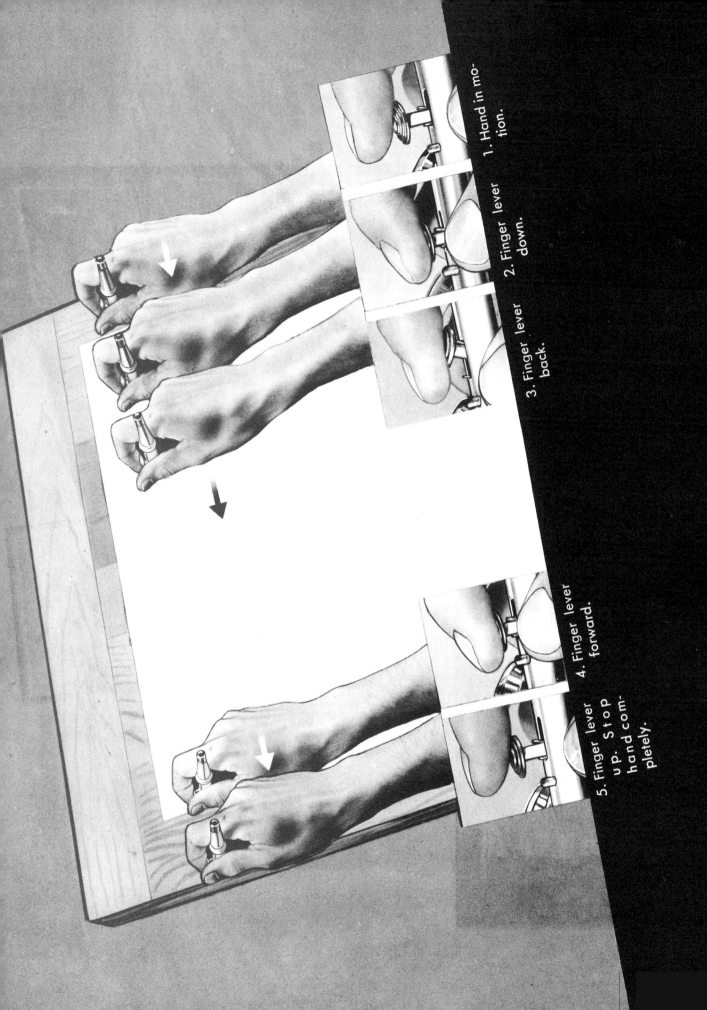

1. Hand in motion.

2. Finger lever down.

3. Finger lever back.

4. Finger lever forward.

5. Finger lever up. Stop hand completely.

Airbrush Line Work

This particular exercise has three objectives: directing the pattern where desired; judging the proper distances between hand and paper; determining how far to pull back on the finger lever. The last two actions govern the size of the spray pattern.

Broad Line: With a pencil, rule off on drawing paper a series of horizontal lines about one inch apart. Starting with the top line, and holding the airbrush about five inches from the paper in a vertical position, aim the airbrush at the line so that the spray pattern will be centered over it. Pull back on the finger lever far enough to give a very broad pattern about two inches in width. Proceed evenly across the page, following the line. Release the paint and air at the end of the stroke. Repeat this in the opposite direction on the second pencil line. Continue until the page is covered. Do not go over any line more than once. Try to make the pattern of uniform width on each stroke.

Medium Line: Using a clean sheet of paper ruled off in the same manner, hold the brush about two inches from the paper and, again directing the pattern at the center of the line, airbrush a pattern about a quarter of an inch wide across the paper. Try to keep the pattern uniform in width and centered over the pencil line. In this exercise the finger lever will not be pulled back as far as in the previous one. It is necessary to acquire proper coordination between the pull on the finger lever and the distance from the paper, and to learn to pull back the same distance on the lever each time, in order to get a pattern of consistent width for each stroke.

Fine Line: Holding the brush as close to the paper as possible, and pulling back very, very slightly on the lever, try to follow the pencil line carefully with a pattern of about the same width. Proceed down the paper in opposite directions, as before. It might be helpful to allow the little finger to rest on the paper, sliding along on its tip, thus serving as a guide. These same exercises may be done with vertical lines instead of horizontal and also with diagonal lines. It is also a good idea to alternate later, so that a broad line, a medium line and a fine line are done one after the other.

"Trouble Shooting"

Grain: If the pattern becomes very grainy, it is generally because the pigment has not been diluted sufficiently with water. Start over again with more dilute color. Grain may also be due to an accumulation of paint on the airbrush tip, to low air pressure, or to a bent needle. See page 154.

Paper Buckling: If the paper blisters or buckles, the paint is too dilute, or too much paint is being applied to the paper during each stroke. In the first instance, add more pigment to the color; in the second, do not pull back so far on the finger lever when airpainting.

Blobs: If large spots of paint occur at the beginning of each stroke, you are releasing the paint before the hand is in motion. If the blob is at the end, you are not allowing the finger lever to move forward at the end of the stroke, thus shutting off the paint supply.

Flared Strokes: This is caused by not moving the whole forearm across the paper when making strokes but merely turning the wrist in order to reach the edges of the paper. Make the stroke with the forearm moving across the paper.

Centipede Effect: This is caused by airpainting too close to the paper and pulling back too far on the finger lever. If a fine line is required, work close to the paper but pull back only very slightly on the finger lever; or raise the hand higher, thereby getting a broader pattern.

Spatter: Fairly large specks of color at the beginning of a stroke are generally caused by having allowed the finger lever to "click" forward too abruptly at the end of the previous stroke. The finger lever should be allowed to return to its normal position gently. Check for clogging.

Curved Strokes: Curved strokes are caused by dipping the hand down towards the paper. The hand should be kept at a uniform distance from the paper during a stroke, except where a line of varying width is desired.

Fig. 1

Fig. 2

Flat Wash

In the previous lesson we airpainted directly on the drawing paper without using a mask. However, most airbrush work is done using either a paper mask or a frisket to protect that portion of the paper which is not to be airpainted. We shall first use a simple paper mask and resort to friskets and other masks later.

FIG. 1. Using a sheet of drawing paper, mark off a 2-inch border on all four sides. Cut out the center section with a razor blade using a metal edged ruler as a guide. Using the *border section* as a mask, place it over another clean sheet of drawing paper.

FIG. 2. Tape the mask to the paper with masking tape, allowing the tape to overlap the paper underneath by about an eighth of an inch. Be certain that the tape is pressed firmly against the paper, otherwise paint may seep underneath. It is now possible to airpaint in such manner that the paint starts and stops on the mask, allowing complete paint coverage on the exposed area of the drawing paper. We are going to airpaint a flat, even tone over this exposed area, producing what is known as a "flat wash." The wash can be of any degree of lightness or darkness. We shall airpaint approximately a 50 per cent gray tone, which would be half-way in value between solid black and white.

Fig. 3

Fig. 4

Fig. 7

FIG. 3. Following the operations instructions given on page 32, airpaint a tone across the top of the exposed area of the paper. Aim the pattern so that its top portion overlaps the masking tape, to avoid a light streak at the top of the wash. Start the hand in motion at the left outside edge of the mask and pull the finger lever back while still over the mask so that the full strength of the pattern falls on the exposed portion of the paper. Do not allow the finger lever to move forward again until the tape on the other side of the page has been reached.

FIG. 4. Now return the stroke from right to left. Allow this second stroke to overlap the first one in such manner that no streak will show. Continue down the page as illustrated.

FIG. 5. Allow the last stroke to overlap the bottom strip of masking tape. This first passage should be kept very light in value.

Fig. 5

Fig. 6

FIG. 6. Now, start at the top again, covering the previous wash in the same manner. It may be necessary to repeat this performance 3 or 4 times over the entire area until a wash of the desired value is reached.

FIG. 7. Before removing the mask, be certain that the paper and tape are dry. Do this slowly so that the tape will not damage the surface of the paper to which it is adhering. (The same mask may be used over again on another sheet of paper, merely by pressing it down around the edge.)

FIG. 8. Removal of the mask reveals a flat, even wash with a clean 2-inch border all around. It might be necessary to practice this wash several times before satisfactory results are achieved. Do not be discouraged by the first attempt, as control of the airbrush is primarily a matter of practice.

Fig. 8

Fig. 1

Fig. 2

Graded Wash

We shall now airpaint a graded wash, which differs from a flat wash in that it changes in value from pure white at the top of the page to solid black at the bottom. The change in value over this area should be a gradual, rather than an abrupt transition from black to white.

FIG. 1. We shall start at the *bottom* of the area, as this is to be the darkest portion.

FIG. 2. Proceed as with the first passage of the flat wash, except that you will progress from the bottom to the top in this particular exercise, and,

FIG. 3. allow the paint to fade off completely *before* reaching the top of the exposed area of paper. Though you may not notice

Fig. 5

Fig. 3

Fig. 4

any deposit of paint on this area, it will build up unless you stop well short of the top.

FIG. 4. Now return to the bottom and proceed as before except that instead of carrying the pattern up as far as on the previous passage, you will stop just short of it, allowing the tone to fade out as shown in [FIG. 5]. It may be necessary to repeat this procedure at least six times, remembering to stop short of the previous application each time. Since the paint is used very dilute for the gray tones, it might be advisable to make it a little thicker by adding more pigment to the solution for the last few passages at the bottom. The finished wash should appear as in [FIG. 6]. Note that the top is white and the bottom black, with a smooth, gradual transition between.

Fig. 6

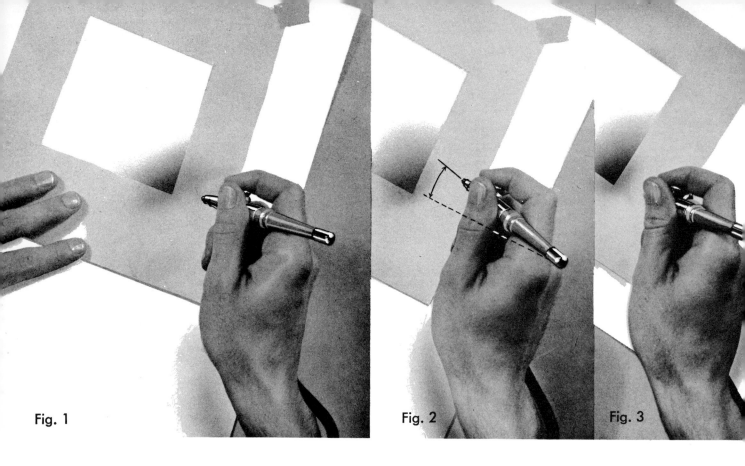

Fig. 1   Fig. 2   Fig. 3

Spotlight Effect

FIG. 1. To create the spotlight effect illustrated, cut out a paper mask with a 4-inch square opening and lay this over a sheet of clean drawing paper. Tape it to the paper at the outside corners so that it will not shift. With one corner facing you, airpaint horizontally across it once or twice. Be certain to aim in such manner that most of the pattern falls on the mask at this corner.

FIG. 2. With the arm in the same position, bend the wrist upwards so that the pattern is raised slightly. Note the change in angle of the airbrush.

FIG. 3. Now return to the original position, airpainting in the corner again. Only about two strokes are made in each position at this time.

FIG. 4. Turn the paper around so that the second corner is nearest to you and airpaint in the same manner in this, and then in each of the other corners.

FIG. 5. Return to the starting corner and airpaint about a half-inch of the corner solid black, fading gradually into the light area. Thus all the corners are kept light until the very end, when the black is added.

FIG. 6. After all corners have been satisfactorily painted, join them with a light tone along the edge of the mask. Remove the mask.

FIG. 7. The center of the spotlight should be as white as possible and only one half-inch of each corner a solid black. The transition should be smooth and gradual.

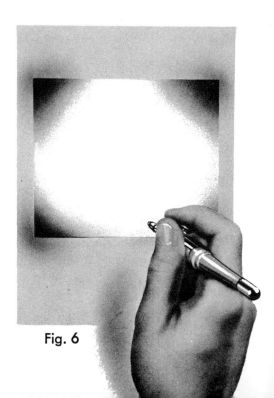

Fig. 6

42

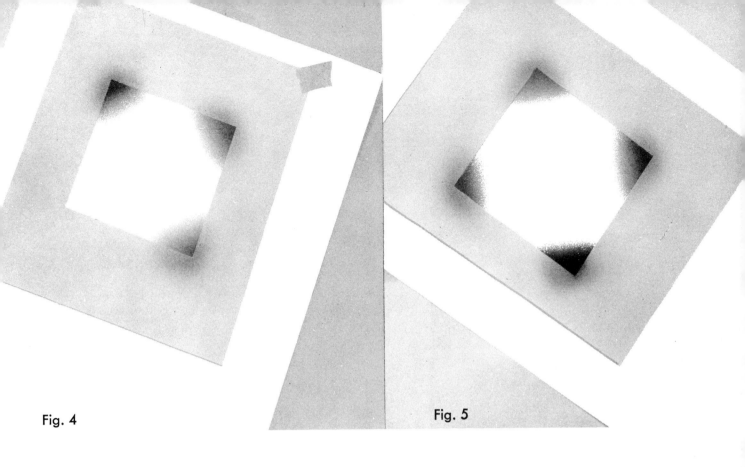

Fig. 4

Fig. 5

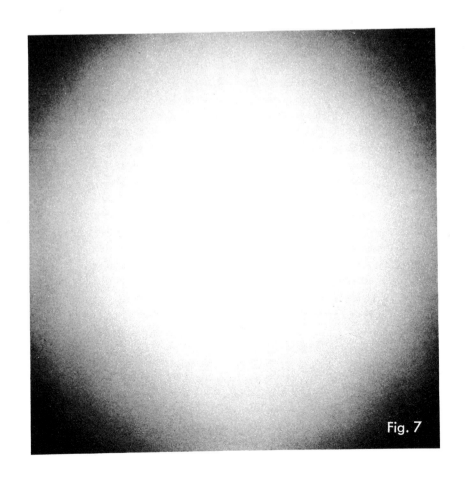

Fig. 7

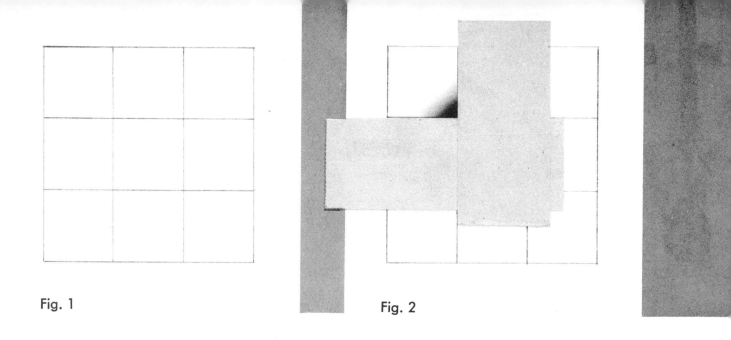

Fig. 1

Fig. 2

Checkerboard Exercise

FIG. 1. Draw a series of 1-inch squares, three across and three down, as illustrated.

FIG. 2. Mask the top left square with two strips of paper overlapping. In the lower right

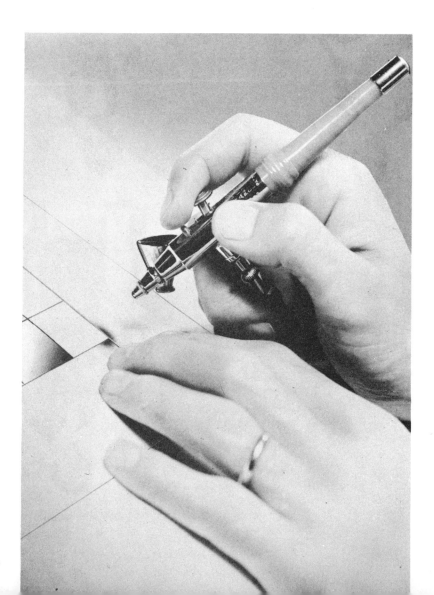

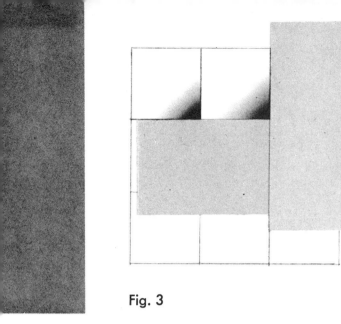

Fig. 3

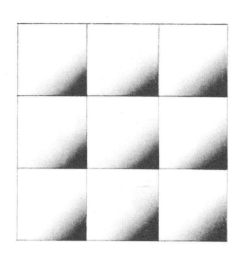

Fig. 4

corner of this top square airpaint a small graded tone, just as was done in the corner of the previous spotlight exercise. Do not allow the color to reach the center of the square. Remember to apply most of the pigment to the corner itself. A closeup of this action is shown below.

FIG. 3. Proceed across the page, then down the page in this manner until the lower right half corners of all squares have been airpainted [FIG. 4].

FIG. 5. Now turn the layout upside down and proceed to airpaint the diagonally opposite corners in the same manner as before.

FIG. 6. The finished exercise shown with the mask removed. Each square should be uniform in shading. This is an excellent exercise for controlling tone and for working close. It is important not to allow the paper to get wet when painting in the corner or the paint will seep underneath the mask. If it does get wet, blow air over the area to dry it out before proceeding.

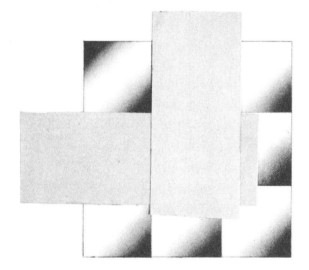

Fig. 5

Fig. 6

a Man's Coffee

White Rose COFFEE

...and Women Love it !

John Ballantine
Cecil & Presbrey, Inc.
Seeman Bros. Inc.

Minor applications of the airbrush are shown in these three illustrations. Nevertheless, where it has been used its effectiveness is evident, as in the blending of the shadow on the man's face, at left, and the smooth blend of the shadows on top of the can. For such purposes a frisket is best employed, as shown on the following pages. The granular effect, indicating the "white heat" in the STEEL poster, is known as spatter. This can be done by airbrush as explained on page 88. The light portions of the ears, snout and spool in the very clever Zwicky poster could be airpainted, using only paper masks. Linework, such as whiskers and mouth, would then be drawn with the handbrush.

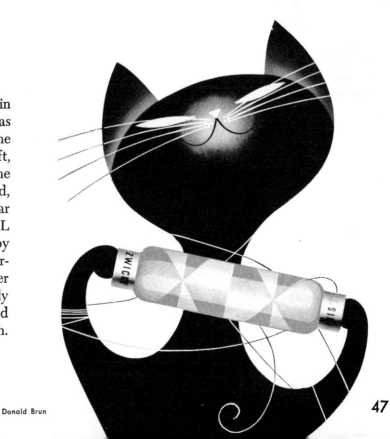

Friskets

So far we have used simple paper masks to protect areas when airpainting. Although masks may be cut in more complicated and irregular patterns to conform to specific shapes, such as the outline of the man's face in the White Rose ad on the previous page, it is more practical to use the frisket method for such purposes. A piece of transparent paper may be coated with rubber cement and adhered to the drawing, enabling the artist to cut out and expose intricate areas for airpainting. A special paper, known as frisket paper, is best used for this purpose. Thin tracing paper can also be used in this manner when the shape is large or comparatively simple. Thin, tinted cellophane may also be used, if necessary. The methods of making, applying, and cutting friskets are shown on the following pages.

Frisket Paper: Asco frisket paper, thin or medium weight, is used. Do not purchase more than a couple of months' supply at a time as the paper turns yellow and brittle. "Prepared frisket papers" are available, already coated with cement.

Rubber Cement and Dispenser: Rubber cement is used for making friskets, as well as for mounting paper, photos, matts, etc. A good grade of cement is important as there is nothing so exasperating as a frisket that does not stick. Obtain white rubber cement that retains its adhering properties even when thinned out considerably with rubber cement solvent. The combination dispenser jar and brush is used to store and apply the cement. This container reduces evaporation of the solvent and also permits the brush to be moved up or down so that only the hairs of the brush are in the rubber cement. Use at least a pint size container with a thick, ¾ inch brush.

Frisket Knife: The frisket knife should be chosen with care. Above all, it should have a good hard steel blade so that it will not require constant sharpening. It should have a round handle so that it will turn easily between the thumb and forefinger when cutting curves. It should be light and balance well in the hand. Shown on page 23 are several types of frisket knives. The first has a permanently mounted blade of the shape generally made for frisket knives. This is also available in a replacement blade model. The second is an X-acto knife, with a small triangular shaped blade. The third is the swivel type knife preferred by some artists for cutting curved areas. It can be locked in position for cutting straight lines.

Making a Rubber Cement Pickup

To remove excess rubber cement from the paper when using a frisket or doing pasteups, it is advisable to use a so-called "pickup," rather than an eraser. This can be made by slopping rubber cement thickly all over the outside surface of the rubber cement jar, then rolling the dry rubber cement into a ball. Use this "pickup" by rubbing gently.

To make a temporary pickup, tear a piece of masking tape off a roll and bend it back upon itself so that the tacky surface remains on the outside and press the ends together. This type of pickup should be discarded frequently as it is likely to scratch the paper surface if used too much.

 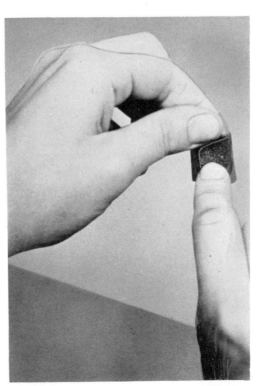 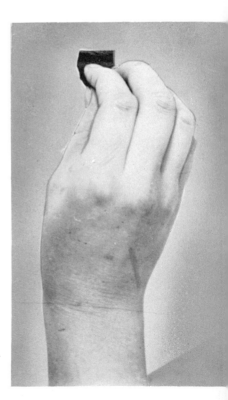

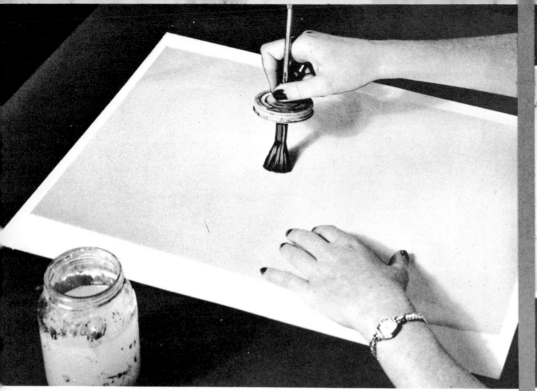

Making a Rubber Cement Frisket

A piece of frisket paper larger than the area to be airpainted should be prepared. Either side can be used. Dab a little rubber cement in each of the four corners of the frisket, then turn it over and flatten it down on a clean piece of cardboard. Starting at the top, brush the rubber cement evenly and smoothly across the frisket paper in both directions until the entire sheet is covered. Allow this to dry, then apply a second coat, gently, over the first

From the center, gently flatten out the frisket paper with the hands or a triangle.

When the second coat has dried, lift the frisket carefully, turn it over so that the coated surface is face down, and place it slowly over the drawing. Allow the center portion to make contact with the paper first, as shown, then the ends.

With the frisket knife, cut through the frisket, but not through the paper beneath it. When cutting straight lines use the steel edge as a guide.

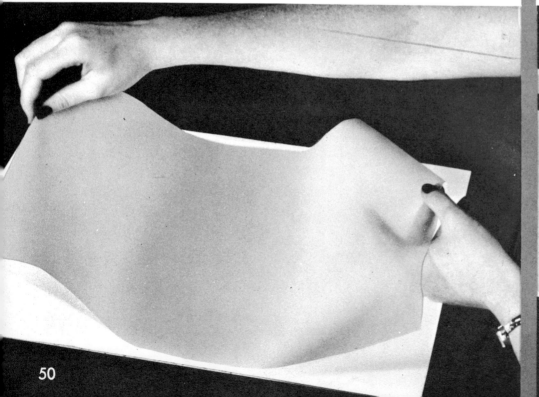

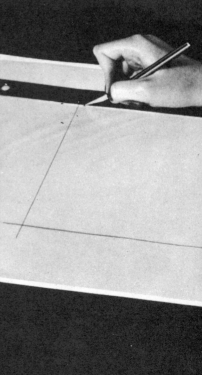

Lift one corner of the frisket; then carefully remove the frisket from the area to be airpainted.

With a pickup, gently remove any rubber cement which may have remained on the paper, being especially careful along the edges of the frisket.

The exposed area of the paper is now ready for airpainting. Where a fairly broad pattern is being applied, as in this instance, sufficient frisket should be allowed for protection of the paper from the paint at the beginning and end of each stroke. On very large jobs it may be advisable to use tracing paper beyond the edge of the frisket paper as an economy measure.

After the required airpainting has been done, remove the frisket. Both paint and frisket should be dry when this is done. Remove any remaining rubber cement from the border of the paper with the pickup.

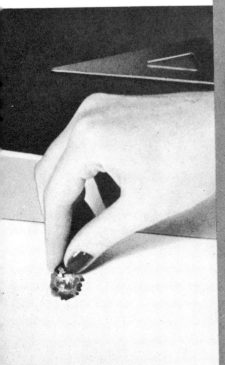

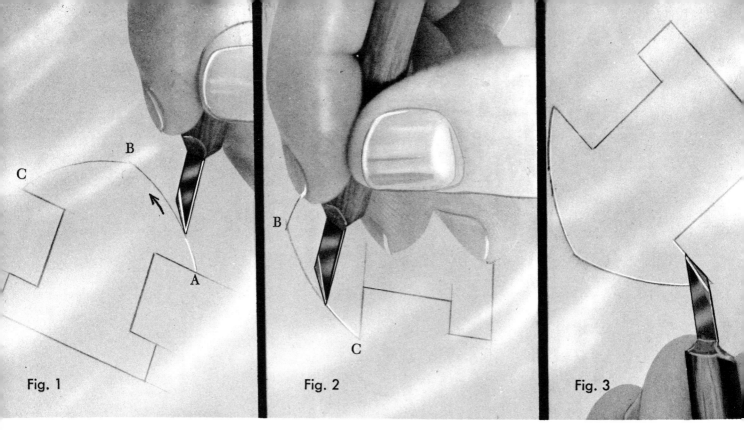

Fig. 1   Fig. 2   Fig. 3

Frisket Cutting

Since frisket paper is very thin and fragile, extreme care must be exercised in cutting the frisket. It is essential that the knife be absolutely sharp and that the frisket paper be firmly cemented to the artwork. The cutting is done only with the toe of the blade. The blade should be sharp enough so that the weight of the knife itself is practically sufficient, without the exertion of any additional pressure. The blade should be held perpendicular to the paper while cutting. For all straight lines use a metal-edged ruler as a guide when cutting. Curved lines can be cut freehand or with the use of a french curve, care being taken not to cut the instrument.

The procedure in cutting an area involving several small angles is shown in these illustrations. The general procedure is to cut towards the apex of the angle, where one side of the angle has already been cut. [FIG. 1] Starting at any point, "A," cut a line as indicated, proceeding in the direction of

A pair of tweezers can be used effectively in lifting the frisket from small areas, instead of using the knife and fingers. This allows better visibility and more delicate control.

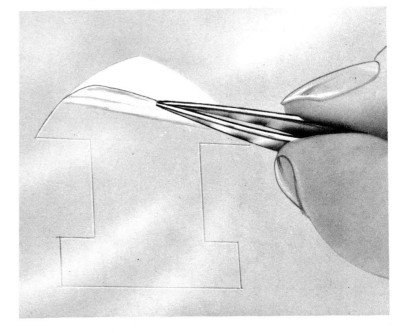

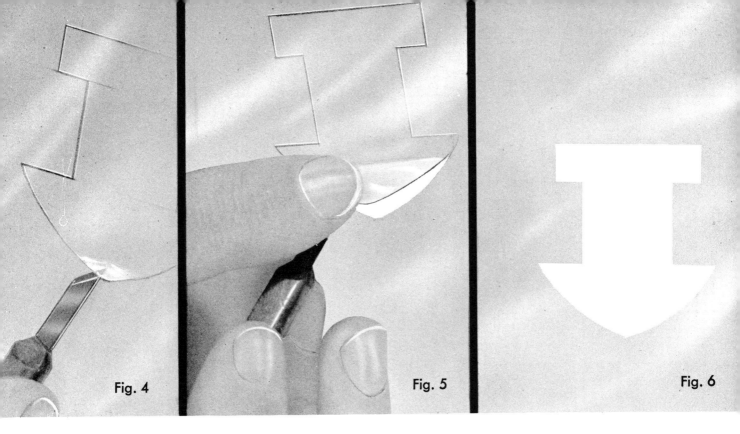

Fig. 4

Fig. 5

Fig. 6

the arrow. [FIG. 2] Now, instead of continuing this cut, turn the drawing around so that the next cut can be made from "C" towards the apex of the angle, "B." [FIG. 3] Again starting at the uncut end of the line, proceed toward the apex of the next angle. Use of the ruler has been eliminated here to simplify the illustration. For the same reason the blade does not appear perpendicular to the paper. [FIG. 4] After all lines have been cut, gently slip the blade of the knife under the frisket paper at one of the corners. [FIG. 5] Place the index finger of the other hand over the frisket paper so that it is held firmly between the index finger and the point of the blade. Lift it gently away from the drawing paper. Watch the edges of the frisket carefully so that any uncut sections can be noted before the frisket paper tears. [FIG. 6] Remove any remaining rubber cement from the exposed area with a rubber cement "pickup," taking care not to lift any corners of the frisket paper.

When cutting circles (not ovals or ellipses), a frisket knife blade can be inserted in the lead holder of a draftsman's compass. A piece of tape or paper should be placed over the center of the circle before inserting the compass point, otherwise a visible hole will be left in the illustration. An alternative to this type of compass is the beam compass, which can also be used with a cutting blade.

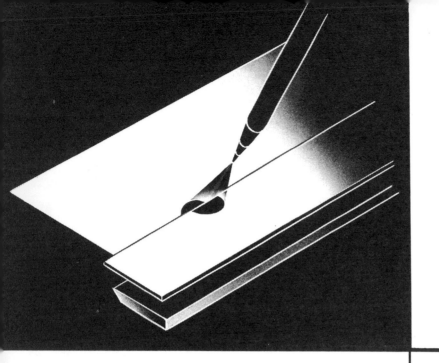

When airpainting a line or area whose bottom edge is fairly abrupt and whose top edge fades out gradually, the airbrush can be first directed almost at right angles to the paper, as shown in this illustration. Keep in mind that the effect is not achieved with one stroke and that the tone should be built up gradually. See the next step.

Use of Raised Mask

When making airbrush strokes whose top and bottom edges vary in gradation of tone, it is possible to use a raised mask to achieve such an effect. This is of special value to beginners where complete freehand control over the airbrush has not yet been acquired. This situation occurs in the shadow of the cylinder shown on page 59. When airpainting such a shadow, a beveled edge ruler can be placed upside down on the paper and a white blotter placed over this so that it is raised from the paper. Holding the blotter down firmly and evenly with the left hand, the pattern can be directed along the edge of the blotter and on the paper at the same time. Depending upon the closeness of the brush to the blotter and the angle at which the pattern is directed, various effects can be achieved, as shown on the next page. Be certain that the blotter has a straight, clean-cut edge, as any irregularities in its edge will affect the airbrush tone. This type of fade-out is known as a "soft" edge, as compared with the "sharp" or "hard" edge obtained by using the mask in contact with the paper. See page 72.

To extend the top edge so that it fades out more gradually, decrease the angle of the brush to the paper, keeping the brush at the same height as previously, and make two or three passages. The combination of these two steps was used in the bottom shadow of the cylinder previously mentioned.

If a *narrow* line is desired, with a fairly *sharp edge* at the bottom and a fadeout at the top, point the brush directly at right angles to the blotter and work much closer to the blotter, as shown in this illustration. This is the method by which the top shadow on the cylinder was achieved.

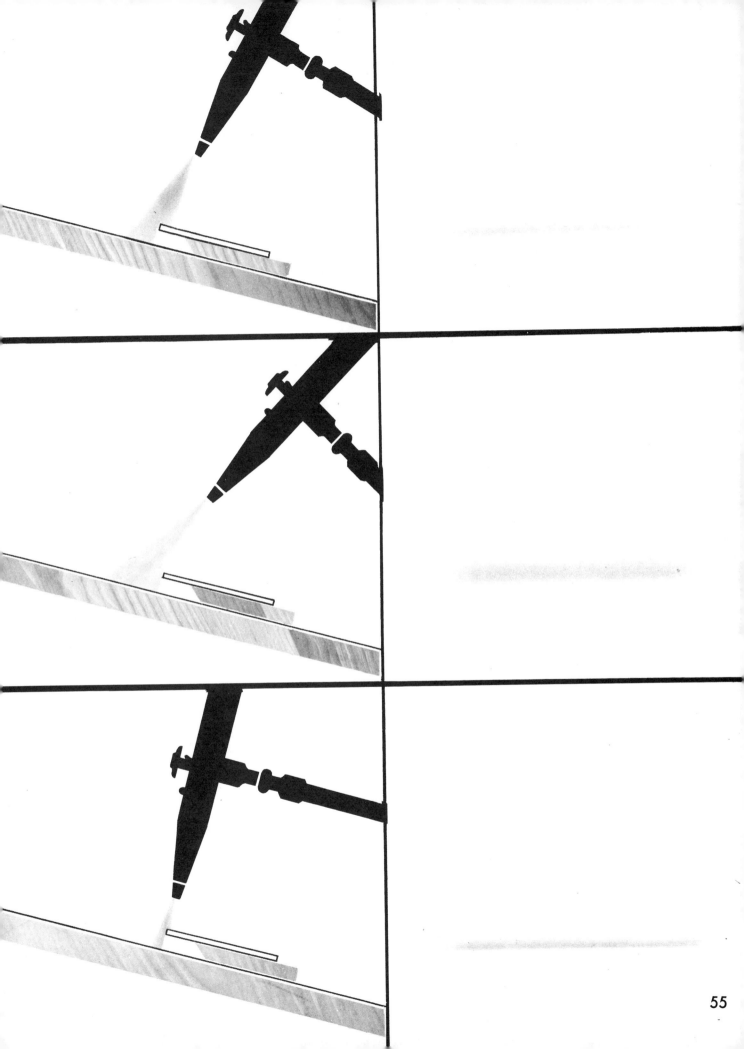

Rendering Basic Forms

Rendering Basic Forms

Rendering of the basic forms; the cube, cylinder and sphere, serves a double function; it provides instruction in procedure — the sequence and types of actions involved in more complicated applications of the airbrush than we have hitherto considered; and it provides a method of shading, or indication of the three-dimensional character of these basic forms of which almost any object is composed. For these reasons, a complete breakdown of procedure is presented. Since to date we have only worked with lampblack pigment used transparently, this method is used here in rendering the basic forms. It is advisable to render the same forms with opaque color later, adapting the procedure shown on pages 78 and 79.

In the shading presented, a single light from the upper left at a 45 degree angle is assumed, as this is the standard type used in rendering. Naturally, where rendering requires a light source from a different direction the shading would have to be changed accordingly. Allowance would also be made for differences in texture; for instance, a shiny, stainless steel pipe would not be affected by light in the same manner as a dull, dark cast iron pipe. Nevertheless, this shading method serves as a general basis for such forms.

Rendering the Cylinder Form

FIG. 1. Draw an elevation view of a cylinder, which in outline will actually be a rectangle. Place a frisket over it, extending about an inch beyond its outline. Cut the frisket along the outline.

FIG. 2. Remove the inside of the frisket, exposing the full area of the cylinder. Be certain to clean off all rubber cement which may have remained on the surface of the drawing paper.

FIG. 3. Since it is advisable to leave reflected light at the bottom of the cylinder and

Fig. 1

Fig. 2

Fig. 3

have the shading start with a soft edge, a raised blotter is used as a mask. Airpaint a few strokes, working almost vertically with the brush at the beginning; then, turn the brush upwards slightly to fade the tone out gradually. Do not airpaint too long or too dark at this time, but leave this portion unfinished and start the top shadow.

FIG. 4. To do this, turn the drawing upside down and proceed as with the bottom shadow, except that a narrower reflected light is to be left, so the blotter should not cover as much of the cylinder as in the previous stage. Airpaint most of this shadow with the brush held close and in a vertical position.

FIG 5. Turn the drawing upright again, returning to the bottom shadow. Without using the blotter, and concentrating on the *bottom* section of the shadow, airpaint this area until it is black. It will be necessary to work close so as not to soften the bottom of the shadow too much. (Remember to pull the finger lever back very slightly.) There will be a light drift of color over the reflected light. If it is necessary, return to the top reflected light and airpaint a light tone over that also, without the blotter.

FIG. 6. The Finished Cylinder: Note that the only really black area is at the bottom of the lower shadow, that this fades out gradually to a white highlight about one third of the way down from the top. The top shadow is narrower and lighter than the bottom shadow, and the top reflected light is narrower and lighter than the bottom reflected light.

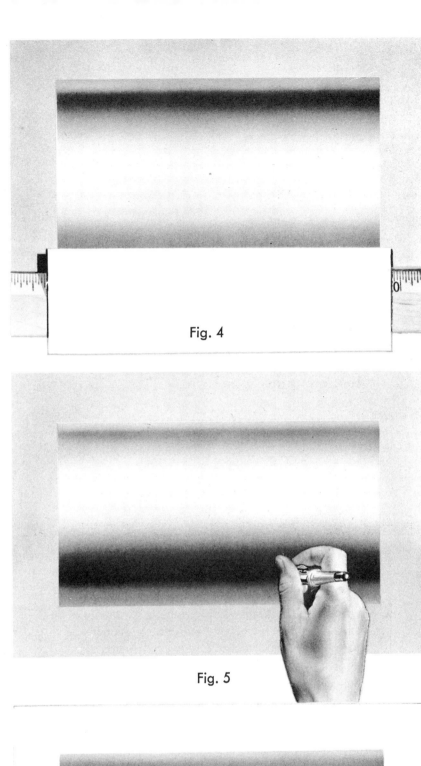

Fig. 4

Fig. 5

Fig. 6

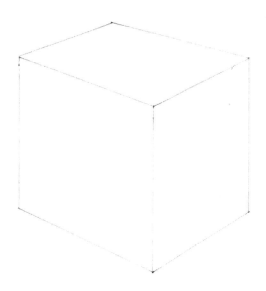

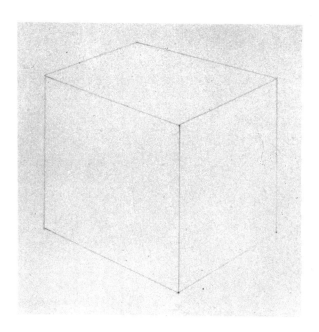

Rendering the Cube Form

The outline of the cube is drawn in pencil. The pencil outline should be dark and sharp to show through the frisket paper.

Place a frisket over the entire cube, allowing sufficient coverage of frisket beyond the cube itself so that the paper will not be soiled when airpainting.

The frisket has been removed from the middle value plane. Again airpaint on the diagonal, but keep as clear as possible of corner "A," as it is desirable to have as much contrast as possible between the three planes intersecting at this point. Do not make corner "B" quite as dark as the black in the first plane. It isn't necessary to cover the first plane.

Remove the frisket from the top plane and again turn the cube around so that the dark corner is nearest you.

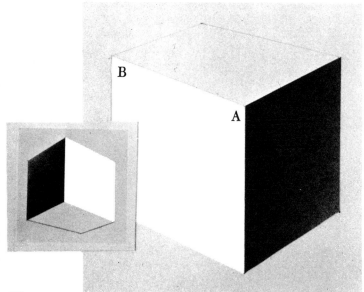

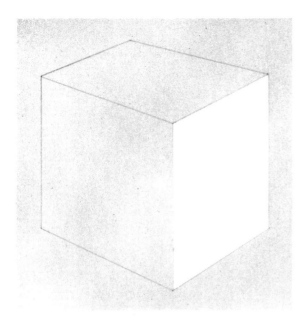

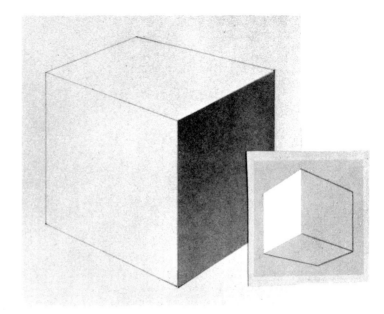

In this particular instance it is desirable to start with the darkest plane as it will serve as a comparative value for the other planes, and also because it will save masking off certain areas when progressing from the darkest to the lighter planes.

Turn the cube around so that what eventually will be the darkest corner is nearest to you. (See insert for position.) Apply the pigment to this corner and fade out to the corner which is diagonally opposite. Start each passage at this dark corner, so that it receives most of the pigment. The darkest tone should not be reached until the very end of this particular operation.

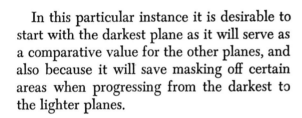

Airpaint only a very light tone diagonally across this corner but be sure to have some tone along both edges. Keep in mind the fact that the values will look much lighter with the frisket on, than will appear after the frisket is removed.

The frisket has been removed. Note that all planes are smoothly graded in value from the darkest corner to the corner opposite. Also that the only black is in the top left corner of the darkest plane and the only white is next to this, and the third corner is halfway in value between the two. The graded tones and contrasting values give a maximum amount of three-dimensional effect.

Rendering the Sphere Form

Draw a circle with the compass and place a frisket over this.

Cut out the circle. This can be done either free hand with the frisket knife, following the circle very carefully, or by using a blade and a compass as illustrated on page 53. Remove the frisket from the sphere, clean off the excess rubber cement and airpaint a very faint tone all around the edge of the sphere, allowing the tone to fall on the frisket also. This should be done in short strokes, working in both directions. Long strokes would be more difficult to control. Try to keep the tone as even as possible, fading out gradually on the inside edge.

Carry this tone up further from the bottom, leaving the highlight, a small circular area at the upper left of the sphere, as white as possible.

Starting in the lower right hand area of the sphere, a short distance in from the edge of the frisket, airpaint a shadow along the right side, then across the bottom and up the left side, as indicated by the arrows. We are now beginning our heavy shading, leaving a reflected light. This shading, as in the previous stage, should be done with short strokes in all directions. When fading out at the upper right and upper left, however, work only in the one direction, indicated by the arrow, as it is easier to fade out in this manner.

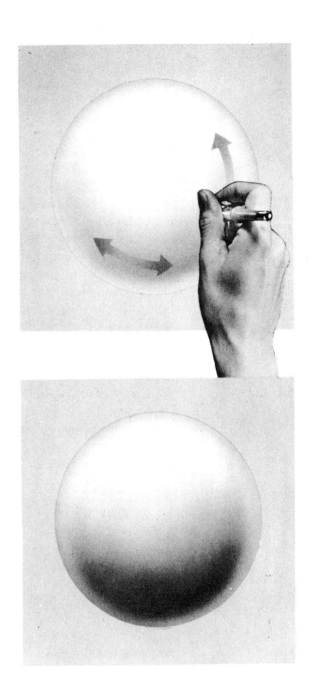

Airpaint a slightly darker tone off the edge of the frisket, at the top of the sphere; then again return to the lower right hand shadow area and continue to darken this. We are now working on our solid black tone, which should be airpainted approximately in the shape of a crescent. The full black is limited to this particular area.

The finished sphere is shown with the frisket removed. Note that the reflected light extends about two-thirds of the way around the sphere. The highlight is in the upper left hand area and the darkest dark is diagonally opposite it in the lower right hand area. The only solid black is the small crescent shape in this area and the tone fades very gradually and smoothly to the highlight. It is possible to work close yet avoid streaks by pulling back very slightly on the finger lever and building up the tones very gradually.

Use of Color with the Airbrush

Although we shall consider the various methods of using color with the airbrush, there is much more to the theory and practice of color than can be covered in a book on airbrush. There are many books on color theory, which can be consulted if necessary.

As with black and white pigments, color can be used in both transparent and opaque form, with the same advantages and limitations for each.

Transparent Colors Liquid dyes are the most transparent colors. They are available in sets of small bottles with individual "eye dropper" dispensers. Dyes are not permanent colors; eventually they fade, especially if exposed to direct sunlight for a lengthy period. However, they are made in very brilliant colors, and when the artwork is to be reproduced in print or film, or used for television, the permanency is not important. Like other colors, dyes can be mixed in the palette to modify each other, or make new colors. For example, a cobalt blue can be made slightly "warmer" by adding a little magenta, or "cooler" by adding a little viridian. More red added to the blue will make a violet or purple. Dyes may be used full strength in the airbrush, as taken from the bottle, or diluted with water to make tints. To make them darker than their full strength either black, or, preferably, their complementary color can be added. Dyes must be carefully and accurately applied as they cannot be easily corrected.

Opaque Color There are various kinds of opaque water colors, known as poster colors, designers colors, gouache and so-called "tempera." Pigments used in delicate airbrushes should be finely ground. They are available in tubes and jars, in paste or semi-liquid form. Artists tube colors may also be used in the airbrush; they are not as transparent as dyes, nor as opaque as the others just mentioned, but are called transparent water colors. Good quality artists colors are permanent. Opaque colors are made lighter, and more transparent, by diluting with water. To retain their opacity they can be lightened with white. Continued airbrushing over an area builds up the color intensity (see color chart at right center, next page) making it denser and more opaque, whether it be a dye or an opaque color.

A simple way to achieve a modified color effect is to trace a drawing on to colored paper, as in the top panel of page 64a, then shade the drawing with black, used transparently where you want the background color to show through, as on the cube. In the third stage of this illustration white is used transparently to highlight the previous stage. Considerable control and effect can be achieved this way, as shown in the illustration of the grinding wheel on page after next. This can be done on a ground of color which has been airbrushed, if you do not wish to use colored paper.

An effective way to use black, white, and one color is to modify the color with black to make it darker and another portion with white to make it lighter. You will thus have black, white, and three shades of a color to work with as in the illustrations at right center.

Still another method is to use india ink transparently to make the drawing as shown on this page, then airbrush dye on the various areas of subject as shown at right. Another version of this is to first airbrush the colors of the various parts in flat opaque then shade each with black. This method is used by Otis Shepard on the next page.

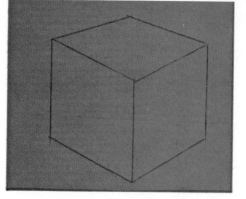

OUTLINE ON COLORED PAPER

BLACK SHADING

WHITE HIGHLIGHTING

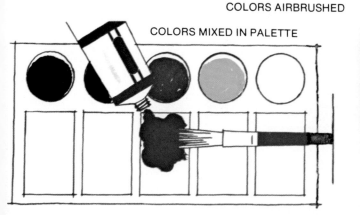

COLORS AIRBRUSHED

COLORS MIXED IN PALETTE

BLACK   DK. BLUE   BLUE   LT. BLUE   COMBINATIO

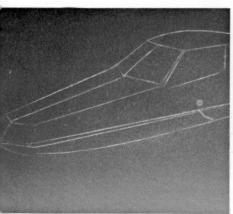

OUTLINE ON AIRBRUSHED
COLOR BACKGROUND

FRISKET ON DRAWING
CUTOUT AREAS AIRBRUSHED

DARKS AIRBRUSHED
FRISKET REMOVED

FAR LEFT: AIRBRUSHED
DRAWING—INDIA INK

CENTER: DYES AIRBRUSHED
OVER EACH UNIT OF DRAWING

LEFT: ALTERNATIVE METHOD—
FLAT OPAQUE COLOR AREAS
OVER WHICH BLACK WATER
COLOR WILL BE AIRBRUSHED

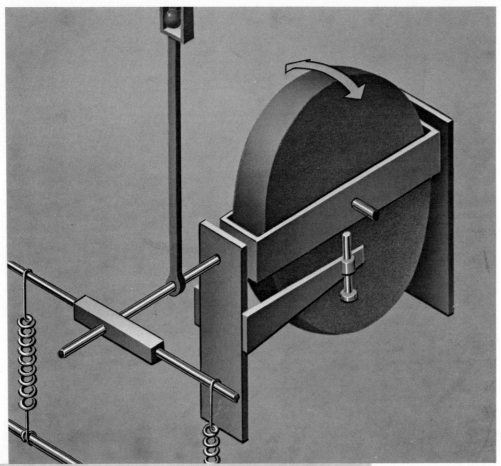

1948 OFFICIAL PROGRAM 10¢

△ An example of black and white pigment airbrushed · semi-transparently on colored background with some hand-brushed linework. Note how ground color shows through on image.

◁ Example of black image airbrushed over solid opaque areas.

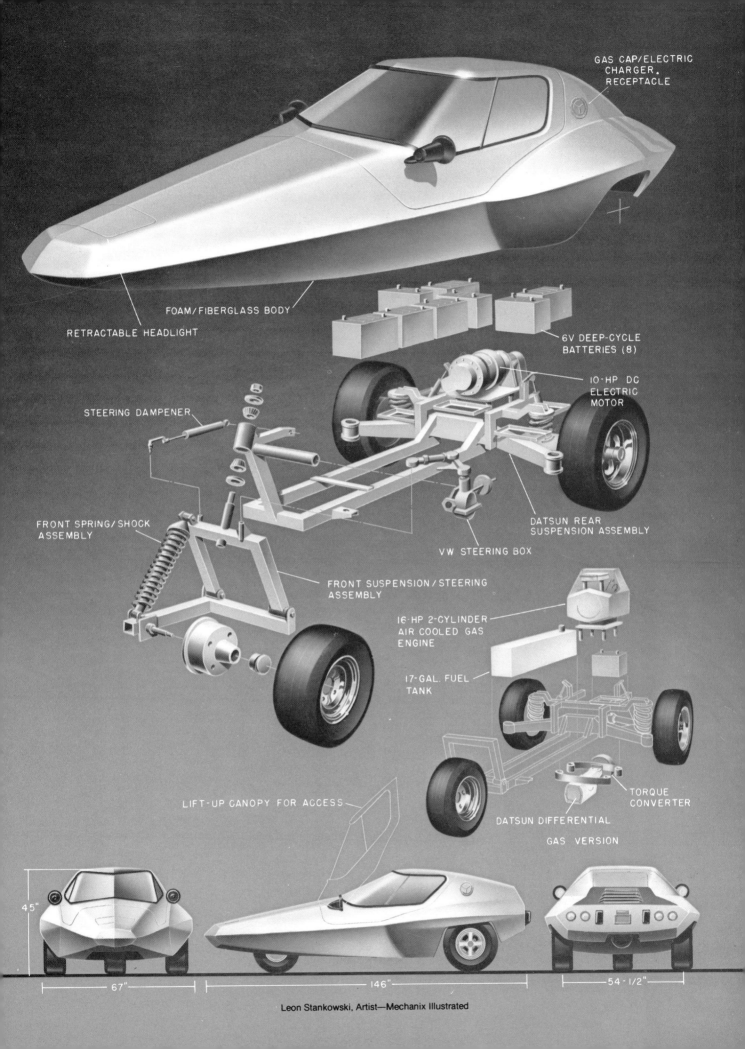

GAS CAP/ELECTRIC CHARGER. RECEPTACLE

FOAM/FIBERGLASS BODY

6V DEEP-CYCLE BATTERIES (8)

RETRACTABLE HEADLIGHT

10-HP DC ELECTRIC MOTOR

STEERING DAMPENER

DATSUN REAR SUSPENSION ASSEMBLY

VW STEERING BOX

FRONT SPRING/SHOCK ASSEMBLY

FRONT SUSPENSION/STEERING ASSEMBLY

16-HP 2-CYLINDER AIR COOLED GAS ENGINE

17-GAL. FUEL TANK

TORQUE CONVERTER

LIFT-UP CANOPY FOR ACCESS

DATSUN DIFFERENTIAL

GAS VERSION

45"

67"

146"

54-1/2"

Leon Stankowski, Artist—Mechanix Illustrated

Airbrush—Transparent Color And Pen Line

The application of simple washes of transparent color over an inked line drawing is illustrated in this project. [Fig. 1] All solid black lines are inked in with a pen, and the black areas handbrushed, using waterproof ink. [Fig. 2] A frisket is placed over the entire drawing, and those areas which are to be dark gray are exposed and airpainted with transparent black. The still darker areas in the compass rose are airpainted more heavily, after masking the adjacent areas. [Fig. 3] This shows, without a frisket, what was done in the previous stage. [Fig. 4] Another frisket is applied, and only the background is exposed and airpainted first with transparent black around the compass rose then with transparent blue, working from the center outwards.

Mechanix Illustrated

Fig. 1

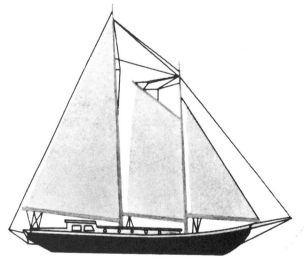

Fig. 2

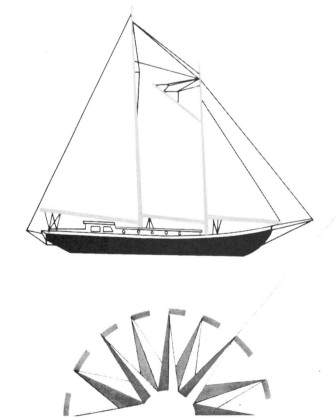

Fig. 3

Fig. 4

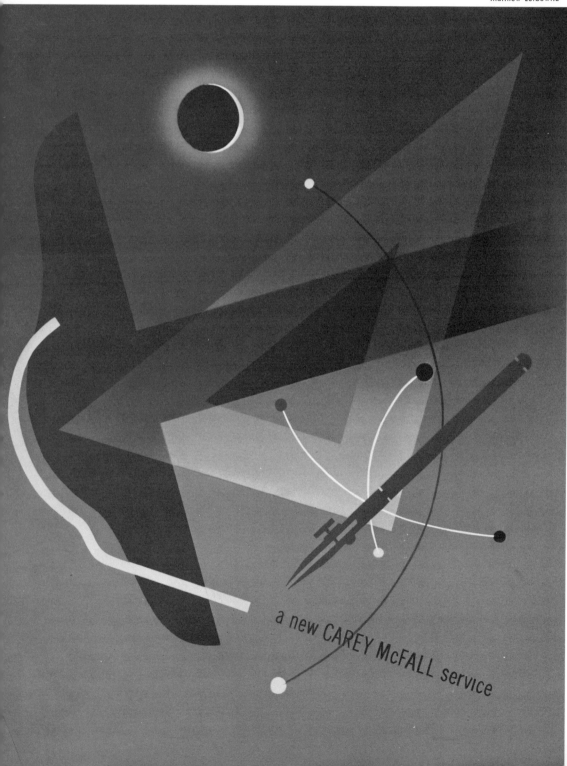

Matthew Leibowitz

a new CAREY McFALL service

The Use of Drafting and Drawing Instruments

Although many aspects of airbrush art fall outside the category of "mechanical" rendering, the application of certain drawing instruments and techniques is helpful in many instances. An otherwise excellent rendering can be lacking in professional finish because the linework, structural drawing, or certain mechanical aspects are improperly executed; therefore, some basic methods are illustrated on the next two pages. These will meet with the needs of all but the artist specializing in the mechanical fields, where the problems are those of drafting, plane geometry, perspective and shadow projection, rather than of airbrush techniques. For further information in such matters, it is best to consult books on engineering drawing, production drawing, drafting, perspective projection, plane geometry and shadow projection.

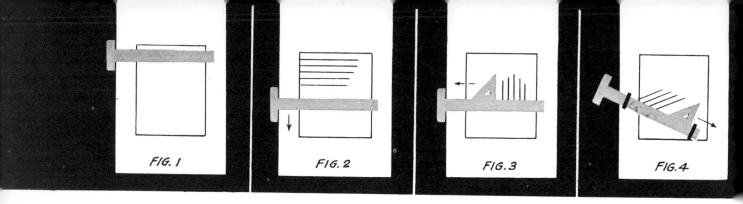

Use Of T-Square And Triangle: [FIG. 1] With the T-square held firmly against the left side of the drawing board, line up the top of the drawing paper with the top edge of the T-square. [FIG. 2] The T-square can thus be lowered to any position for ruling horizontal parallel lines. [FIG. 3] For ruling vertical lines, use the vertical side of the triangle as a guide. [FIG. 4] For ruling parallel lines at other angles adjust the triangle to the desired line, set the T-square against the triangle, then slide the triangle along the T-square in this position.

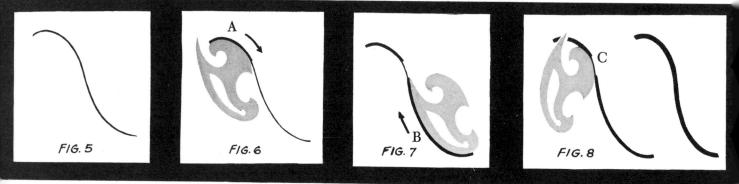

Use Of French Curve: [FIG. 5] A curved line which is to be drawn accurately and smoothly with the french curve is first sketched lightly in pencil. [FIG. 6] Fit a corresponding section of the french curve to the line at "A" and follow the curve with a pencil. [FIG. 7] Move the french curve to "B" and draw this section of the line. [FIG. 8] Now join "A" and "B" with section "C," completing the drawing of the curved line.

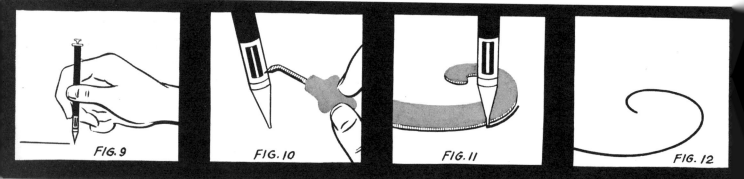

Drawing Ellipses: [FIGS. 9-12] The Wrico pen makes an ink line of uniform thickness. For heavier lines, different size pens are used. The Wrico easily manages curves of short radius. It is filled by means of the ink-stopper and used in a vertical position. [FIGS. 13-15] Acetate ellipse guides are used to draw mechanical ellipses or portions thereof in ink or pencil. The guides are made in different sizes and different degrees of perspective.

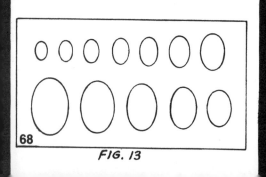

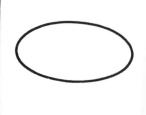

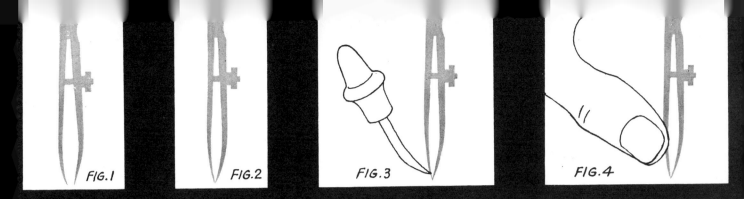

Use Of Ruling Pen: The ruling pen is used with ink or opaque water color to make mechanically straight or curved lines of uniform thickness. [FIGS. 1-2] The thickness of the line can be varied by adjusting the position of the blades of the pen with nut. In open position it will give a thick pen line; in the closed position it will give a thin pen line, with variations between these. [FIGS. 3-4] Fill pen with India ink by means of the filler attached to the bottle stopper. Wipe the excess ink off the outside of the pen.

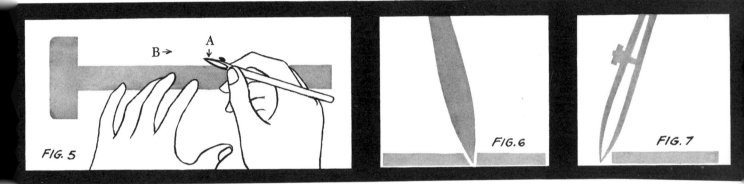

FIG. 5. The pen is used against the side of a T-square for straight lines. The front view, taken from "A," and the side view, taken from "B," [FIGS. 6-7] respectively will clarify the positions of the pen. The same angle should be maintained throughout the stroke. The ruling pen should be kept clean at all times.

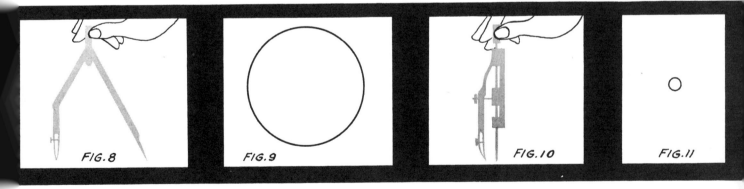

FIGS. 8-9. The pen compass is used to make circles, and [FIGS. 10-11] the "drop compass" is used for very small circles. [FIG. 12] The ruling pen is used with a "french curve" to make accurate curved lines. [FIG. 13] It can also be used with an "adjustable curve" which can be shaped as required.

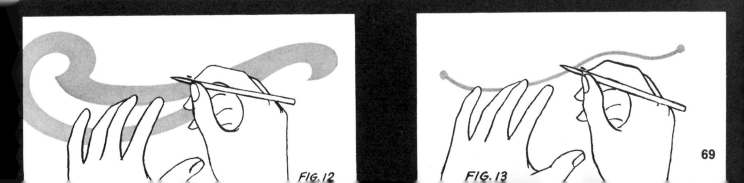

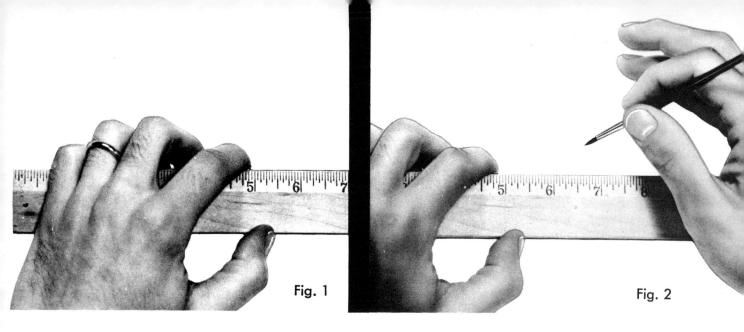

Fig. 1

Fig. 2

Ruling Straight Lines

While possible, it is not always convenient or advisable to rule a straight line with paint in the ruling pen. This especially applies where the line is being drawn on a surface which already has been airpainted with watercolor. There is always the possibility of the line spreading on the painted surface, especially if the pigment in the pen is too thin. The sable brush, used with a ruler, is faster because there is no need to change over to the pen, with its consequent adjusting, cleaning, etc. Also, it allows more control in making straight lines of varying thickness, and small curved lines, using opaque color. India Ink would spread if used over an *opaque* airpainted area.

FIG. 1. A fairly thick ruler with a metal edge is advisable. It should be grasped in the left hand, with only the base of the ruler in contact with the paper, the top raised to an angle of about 30 degrees. This position is better shown in the side-view [FIG. 6]. Be certain that the ruler is level and in firm contact with the paper. [FIG. 2] Hold the brush between the thumb and index finger of the right hand.

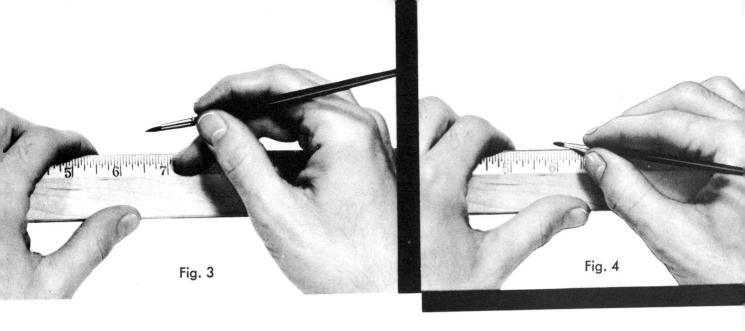

Fig. 3

Fig. 4

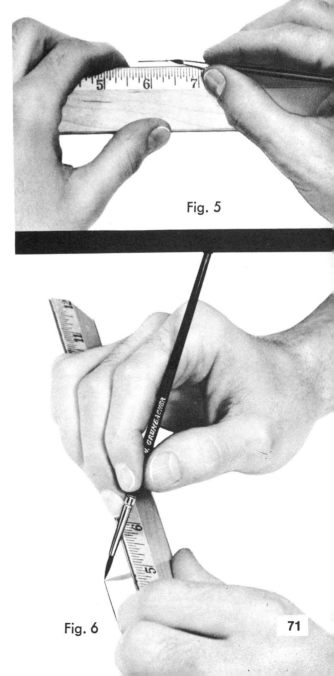

Fig. 5

FIG. 3. Bring the second finger down so that the fingernail is in contact with the top edge of the ruler and free to slide along this edge. The brush is still held only between thumb and forefinger. [FIG. 4] Lower the brush so that the metal ferrule of the brush is in contact with the metal edge of the ruler. With the second finger still touching the edge of the ruler, it should be possible to maneuver the brush freely up or down by bending thumb and forefinger. [FIG. 5] The brush is thus placed in contact with the paper, and moved along the ruler to make the straight line. Pressure on the brush should be even, when a line of uniform thickness is desired, as any increased pressure will result in a thicker line.

By starting out with a light pressure, and increasing the pressure as the hand moves along the ruler, a line of varying thickness, from thin to thick, can be obtained. Throughout this procedure, the brush should be almost perpendicular to the paper, and the angle of the brush with the paper should not be changed throughout the stroke. When making lines with pigment, the paint should be just thin enough to flow off the brush, but not so thin that it will spread. The paint should be thicker than when used in the airbrush.

Fig. 6

Masks

When the outline of an area to be airbrushed is not complicated enough to require the use of a rubber cement frisket, or if for other reasons its use is inadvisable, a mask is used to shield the area from paint. Masks can be made of drawing paper, blotting paper, tracing paper or thin acetate sheets.

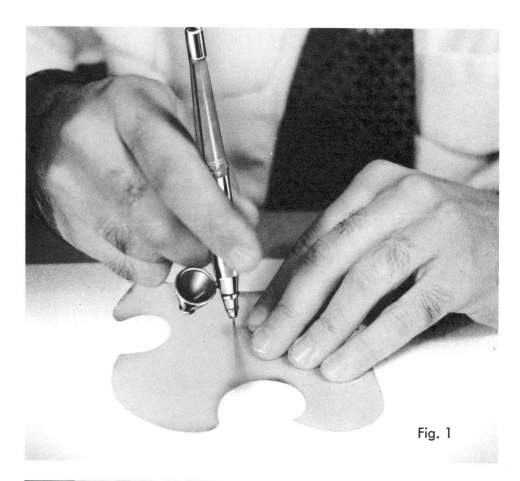

Fig. 1

Clear or frosted acetate of about .0075″ thickness is suitable. The outline of the area to be airpainted is traced. The mask is cut to this shape and placed in direct contact with the photo or illustration to be airpainted, as shown [FIG. 1]. This will result in a sharp-edged airbrush image as shown [FIG. 2]. If a soft or fuzzy edge is required the mask should be raised, as shown on page 54, or held in the hand, as shown [FIG. 3]. An irregular area can be airbrushed in this latter manner by moving the mask to follow the outline of the image while airpainting. Such procedure is useful when airpainting a background around a head, as in a portrait illustration or photo retouch, for in such cases a hard, cut-out effect is objectionable.

The tracing paper mask, unless it is heavy vellum, is used only once for a specific area, as it becomes wet and curls. The acetate mask can be cut in various shapes, as shown on the next page, and thus used as stock masks, singly or in combination, to fit an area to be masked. They can be wiped clean with a damp rag when paint accumulates on them. When using masks, do not work too wet . . . release only a little paint at a time. Direct the paint only *over* the edge of the mask, not *into* the edge.

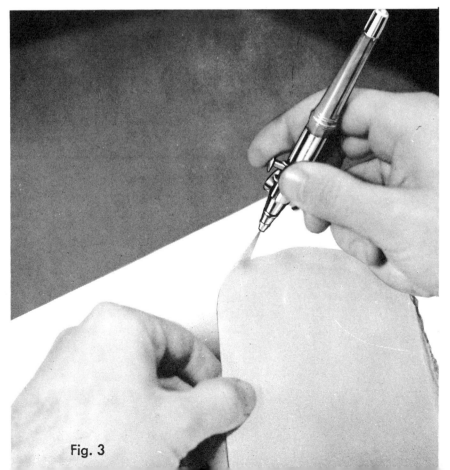

Fig. 3

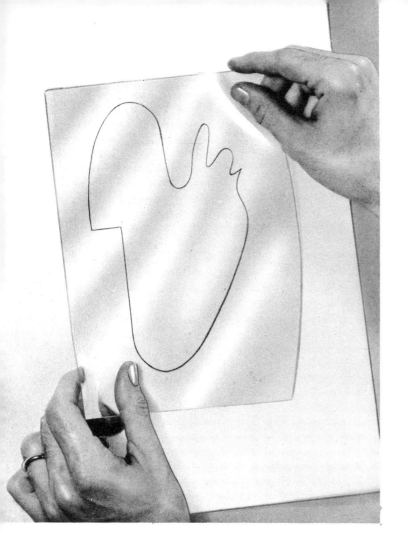

Making a Mask

The desired shape of the mask is drawn in pencil on paper. A sheet of clear or frosted acetate is placed over the drawing. The acetate should be held securely in position by a piece of drafting tape or scotch tape.

The acetate is scored, following the outline of the drawing underneath, with a frisket knife or sharp razor blade. It is not necessary to cut through the acetate. It is important, however, to place the blade in the same cut at the end of each knife stroke so that the cut will be one continuous line. Rotate the acetate and paper so that the curves can be cut in the most convenient position. Use the ruler when cutting straight lines.

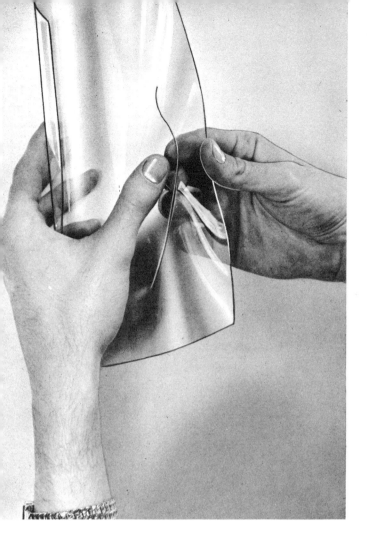
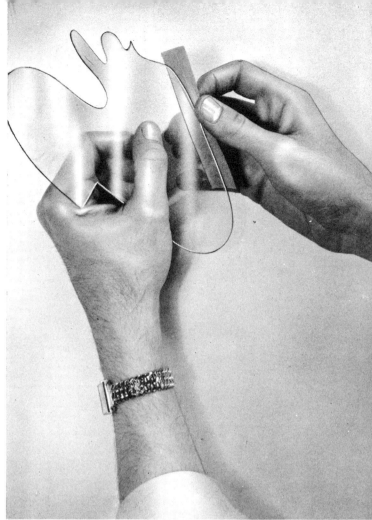

Remove the acetate from the paper. Bend back the acetate as shown above, so that the acetate will crack completely along the cut. Maneuver the acetate as necessary to open up only a short length of the cut at each opening. Be particularly careful around sharp curves and angles.

With a piece of fine sandpaper, smooth the edges of the mask so that all curves are regular and uniform. To get inside of small curves at the base of the finger-like projections in this mask, wrap a piece of the sandpaper around a pencil.

Opaque Retouch Grays

Retouch grays are opaque water colors, supplied in tubes or jars which vary in progressive values from a tone slightly darker than white, to a tone slightly lighter than black. The particular set illustrated here ranges through six values, from No. 1 gray to No. 6 gray. Of a particular brand, such as Grumbacher, Paasche, etc., any tube of No. 1 gray will match, in value, any other tube of No. 1 gray but a No. 1 Grumbacher will not match a No. 1 Paasche. The small blocks of gray, above, show the colors from the corresponding tubes applied solidly, indicating their true tones. No matter how much more may be applied of each particular color over the same area, it will not get any darker. However, in the longer blocks below these, the color has been used semi-transparently. In other words, it has been applied full strength at the top of the block, and allowed to fade out by airpainting less color across the bottom of the block. We refer to this as using an opaque color semi-transparently, though it is a term which may sound confusing. To clarify, if a pencil mark were drawn down the center of each block from top to bottom, before airpainting, it would be obliterated at the top by the heavy opaque color, but would gradually become more visible until it could be seen clearly at the bottom. It should be noted that No. 6 gray is not black and No. 1 gray is not white. Use Grumbacher Lampblack and Gamma White respectively where these tones are required.

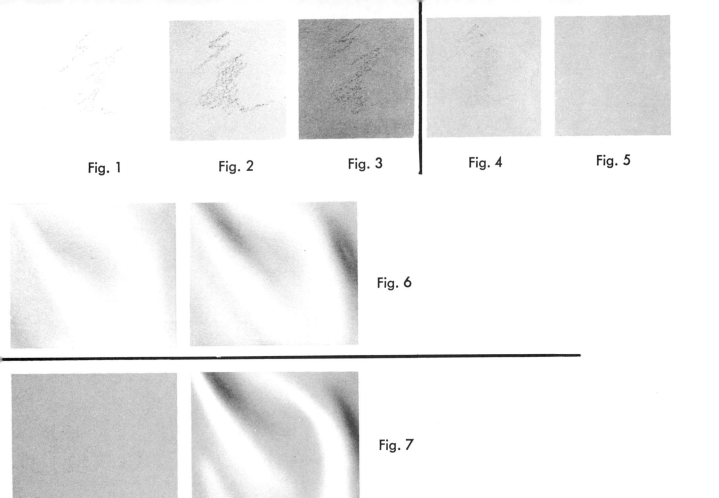

Fig. 1   Fig. 2   Fig. 3   Fig. 4   Fig. 5

Fig. 6

Fig. 7

Transparent and Opaque Pigments

Important characteristics of transparent and opaque pigments, whether black, white or actual colors, are shown here. It is necessary for the student to understand these, as all artwork or photo-retouching will be done by working either transparently or opaquely, or by a combination of both techniques. The ultimate effect desired, the method of approach and the nature of the material or subject matter must be considered.

FIG. 1 shows pencil marks made on white paper. FIGS. 2-3 show progressive stages in airpainting lampblack transparently (diluted) over the pencil marks. Note that only as more paint is applied and becomes darker do the pencil marks begin to disappear, and only when the background value matches the value of the pencil marks will they be obliterated.

FIG. 4. However, using opaque retouch gray No. 3, the pencil marks have begun to fade with only a slight application of the pigment, and [FIG. 5] after heavier application, have disappeared completely. Nevertheless, the background is still a medium value gray — not a black, as would have happened when using transparent pigment.

The difference in working methods between transparent and opaque color is shown, [FIGS. 6-7]. When working transparently, to render an area with strong highlights and shadows we would airbrush only the darks, *leaving* the highlights, [FIG. 6, left]. The shadows could be carefully darkened to the desired values, [FIG. 6, right]. Using the opaque method, [FIG. 7, left], we can first apply a solid tone of middle value gray; then [FIG. 7, right], apply darker grays or black for the shadows, white for the highlights. This allows more control of the shapes and values, and corrections can be made by re-covering with any value desired, whether light or dark.

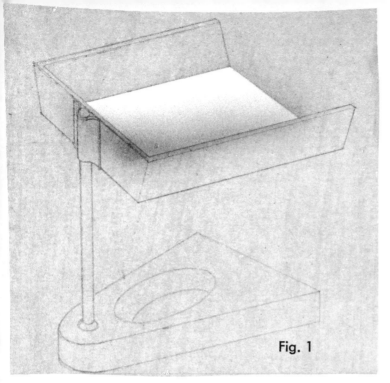

Fig. 1

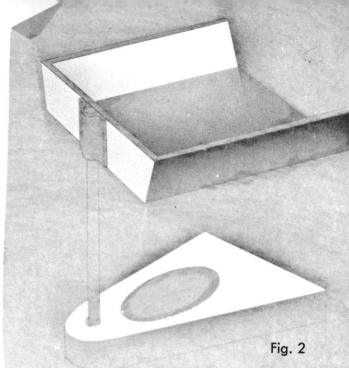

Fig. 2

Comparison of Transparent and Opaque Rendering

Rendering an object, first by the transparent, then by the opaque color method, is illustrated on these pages. The major difference is that in a transparent rendering we start with the white of the paper and gradually build up our darks, whereas in the opaque rendering we may start with a middle value and build up our darks and lights as required.

Transparent Method: [FIG. 1] Remove the frisket from the bottom plane of the tray and airpaint a tone, working it off the edge of the frisket. Leave the upper area of this plane almost white. [FIG. 2] Expose the three side planes of the tray. (Leave the frisket

Opaque Rendering Method: [FIG. 5] By comparison, working with opaques, we leave the frisket only on the background, exposing the entire subject. A medium value tone, a No. 3 gray, is airpainted over this exposed area. It is not necessary to leave any highlights — they can be airpainted with white or light gray as we shade each section. [FIG. 6] If the pencil outline drawing was sharp and dark it will show through this application of No. 3 gray. Using masks or a frisket, shade the planes with a No. 4

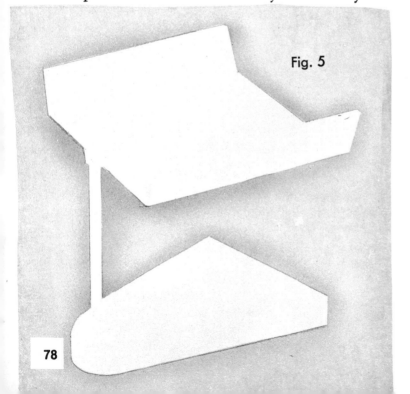

Fig. 5

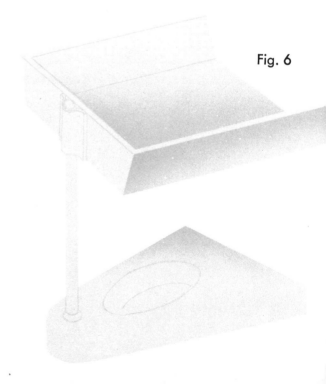

Fig. 6

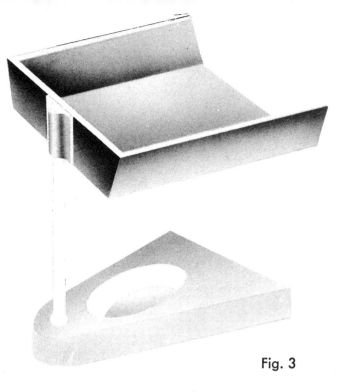

Fig. 3

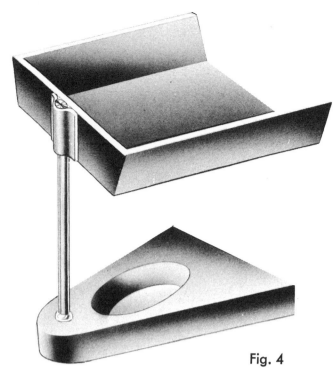

Fig. 4

intact on the narrow *top* edges of these planes as they are to remain white in the finished rendering.) Lightly airpaint a flat tone over all the three planes and then gradually shade each one by applying the paint more heavily, using a mask where necessary. (Since the white area in the bottom plane, done previously, would be darkened by any spill-over, it

is necessary either to cover this with paper or to re-frisket this particular area.)

FIG. 3. Continue with other areas, airpainting the tone over the entire area wherever possible, being careful to leave the highlights; then mask as required to build up the shadows. [FIG. 4] Using a No. 1 sable brush and ruler, add the line work, both dark and light (opaque), to hold the edges.

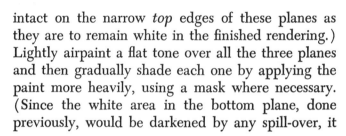

gray. If the gray is applied so heavily that the outline disappears trace it in again on the gray tone.

FIG. 7. Carry this further with No. 5 gray. [FIG. 8]

Add black for the stronger darks and use white or No. 1 gray to fill in the lightest areas. Any corrections or changes can be made by working over with another opaque color.

Fig. 7

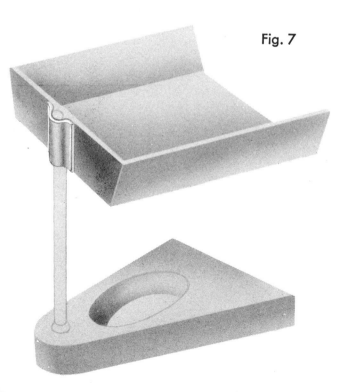

Fig. 8

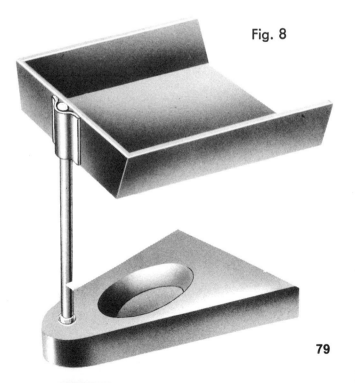

Rendering Projects

The techniques and methods learned in the previous lessons will now be applied to the projects illustrated and explained in this section of the book. Actual job assignments done in the author's studio were selected for this purpose. Some were photographed during the progressive stages of development when the job was being done; others, having been completed before this book was planned, were done over in the same manner as the original. These projects were selected and arranged with a fourfold purpose in mind; to progress from comparatively simple assignments to highly complicated ones; to provide a variety of methods and techniques suitable for every problem; to cover as many diverse fields of airbrush application as possible, and to enable the student to copy them. Although as many step-by-step breakdowns as considered necessary for an understanding of the procedures are shown, one is naturally restricted by the limitations of the book form and the necessity for covering as diverse a range as possible. Where clarity might otherwise have been sacrificed, procedure was changed slightly from that actually used in the original rendering, but expediency of methods and short cuts come with practice and experience; at this stage, imparting the knowledge has to be considered first. Following each project are examples of the work of other artists, or the author, which are related either in technique or subject matter.

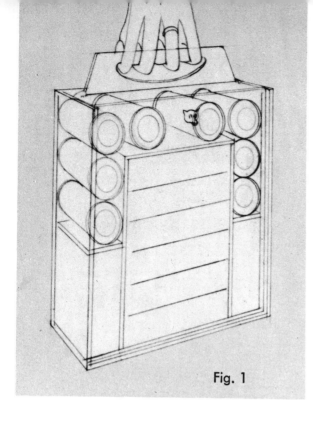

Fig. 1

Product Design

This particular project shows one method of illustrating a newly designed product. The rendering is presented to the client to show the function and appearance of the new design, in this particular instance a plastic container for frozen foods.

Since such work is not usually used for reproduction and is often used merely as a quick visualization, subject to many changes before the final design is settled upon, the rendering must be done quickly and inexpensively.

As there are strong dark and light areas in the packages, combined with a transparent, highly reflective plastic case, this rendering was done on gray paper. This supplied the middle tones for the illustration and offered a good contrasting ground for the

Fig. 3

Fig. 4

plastic. Since the food packages were not shaded, they were painted in with a hand brush. The only air-painting involved is that on the plastic container.

FIG. 1. The outline drawing of the object is done as usual in pencil on tracing paper, and the back of the tracing paper is coated with white chalk for the transfer. [FIG. 2] The drawing is transferred to the gray paper. [FIG. 3] The solid areas of the cans and packages are painted in with opaque water color, using the sable hand brush. The outline of the plastic container is drawn with a ruling pen and white water color paint. [FIG. 4] The lettering is applied with the hand brush and various line details added. [FIG. 5] The container is airpainted transparently with white paint, using paper masks where necessary, as at bottom left.

Fig. 2

Fig. 5

Product And Catalogue Rendering

Quite often it is necessary to illustrate, for reproduction, products which have already been designed but not yet manufactured, or objects which do not conveniently show their construction photographically. In general, a slick photographic effect is desired and this is more convincingly obtained by the use of opaque or semi-opaque color. The cooling unit shown on these pages had to be rendered for catalogue use.

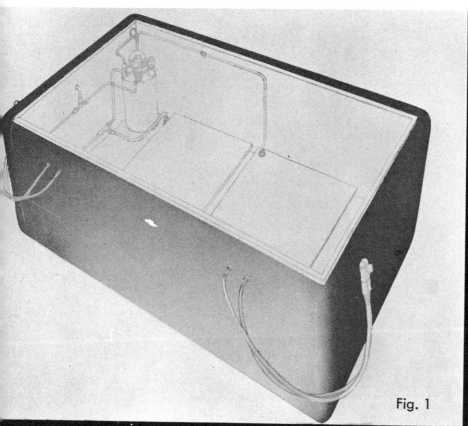

Fig. 1

FIG. 1. A frisket is placed over the pencil drawing and the external portion of the cooler exposed. This is airpainted with a No. 3 gray, used semitransparently, to vary the tone in the front plane. The right-hand plane is then darkened with a No. 4 gray, keeping a soft edge at the near corner.

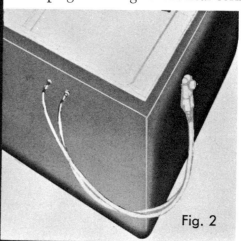

Fig. 2

[FIG. 2] This corner is darkened further with a No. 5 gray, as are the bottom edge of the cooler and the area where the top plane meets the front plane. A guideline for the soft highlight edge can be indicated with opaque white. [FIG. 3] The highlight is gradually airpainted over this line with opaque white used rather thinly. Any deviation in the airbrushed line

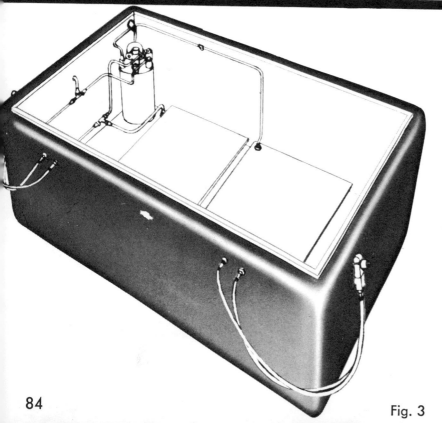

Fig. 3

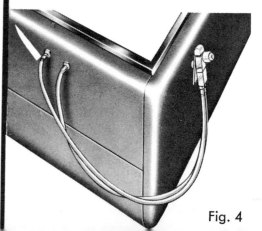

Fig. 4

can be corrected by working back with the dark color. At the fork of the "Y" it is necessary to end the highlight airbrush line rather abruptly. When working an effect such as the *vertical* highlight line, which is strong at the fork of the "Y" and fades out at the bottom, it is advisable to airpaint only in one direction. Start at the fork of the "Y" and work towards the bottom. [FIG. 4] The shadow and highlight lines formed by the joints are ruled, using opaque color. The shadows formed by the hose on the front plane are airpainted, and the frisket now removed from the rendering. Using a new frisket, the rubber sealing gasket is exposed and airpainted as a solid black unit, then flashed with No. 3 and No. 1 gray for highlighting. The No. 1 is placed in the center of the No. 3 highlight area to build up its intensity. Darks and lights are juxtaposed to separate top and side planes of this black gasket. Now this frisket is removed. Handbrush lines, black and white, are added last.

FIG. 5. Everything is covered with a fresh frisket. The two cooler plates on the bottom of the cooler are exposed and flashed (that is, painted in a streaky fashion) with transparent black. The side planes of the interior of the cooler are exposed (the airpainting just completed is protected with paper masks) and are airpainted using a different direction for the flashing. During this operation the pipe-lines are left covered with the frisket. The shadows cast by the pipelines on the walls of the cooler are next airpainted with No. 5 gray. [FIGS. 6-7] After the flat planes have been rendered, the cylindrical unit is frisketed and airpainted as shown in these two illustrations, and all linework completed with handbrush and opaque color.

Selmix Dispensers, Inc.
Pepsi-Cola Co.

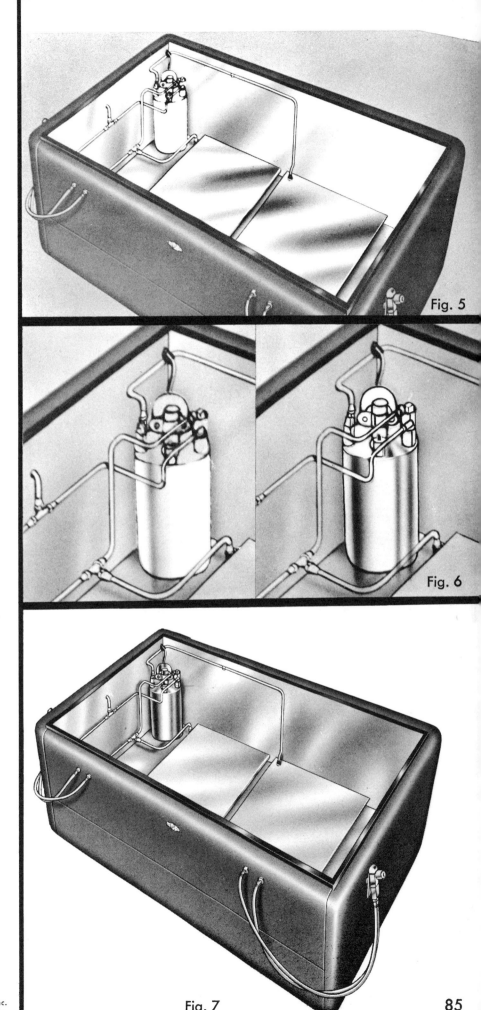

Fig. 5

Fig. 6

Fig. 7

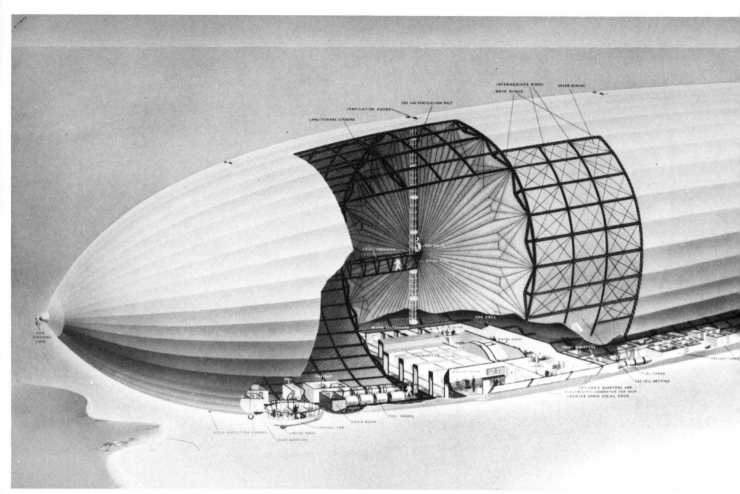

John W. Hauser, *Industrial Designer*

Rolf Klep, *Fortune Magazine*

Drybrush, Stipple and Spatter

Rough textural effects, such as *drybrush,* used in the sky on this page, *stipple,* the coarse water spray on page 109, and *spatter,* the granular effect in the water on the opposite page, may be used effectively as a contrast to the smooth tones of the airbrush. Such effects can be produced directly on the unpainted paper or on areas to which paint has already been applied. Drybrush and stipple are done with the sable or bristle brush, using comparatively thick paint. The hairs of the sable brush are spread by pressing the heel of the brush against a piece of scrap paper with a slight twisting motion. Drag the *tip* of the brush across the paper for the drybrush effect. For the stipple, pat the paper lightly or heavily with the spread tip, depending upon whether a fine or coarse stipple is desired. Spatter is obtained by using the paint thickly in the airbrush, with the pressure lowered sufficiently to give the desired effect. Spatter is less evenly distributed than stipple. The size of the spatter is also increased by raising the airbrush further from the paper.

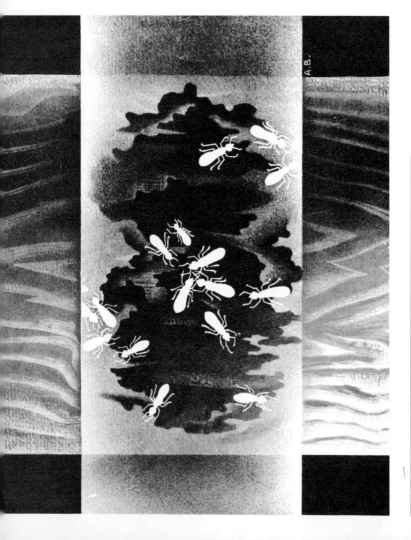

Stencil Technique

Stencil paper has image cut out and space airbrushed.

Cutout from previous stencil is pasted down; airbrush applied over edge for vignette effect.

Walter Bomar
New York Central R.R.

HISTORIC NEW ENGLAND
NEW YORK CENTRAL SYSTEM

See page 96b for full color reproduction of this illustration.

Pictorial Rendering

We may consider pictorial rendering those phases of airbrush art which deal mainly with landscape, still life, figure and portrait subjects. Though friskets may be used, as in mechanical art, more of the airpainting is actually done freehand in pictorial art. In many instances, handbrush art, such as dry brush, stipple or line-work, is also used, for textural effects.

Fig. 1

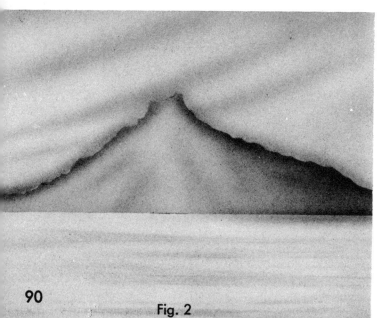

Fig. 2

Fig. 3

Ruth Hilf, *Stylist*
Royaledge Paper Co.

Tropical Scene

This particular illustration is representative of the problems encountered in pictorial rendering. A good general procedure in rendering a subject of this nature is to start with the areas furthest away in the scene and to proceed methodically to the foreground.

FIG. 1. Since the sky and water cover the major area of the illustration and are furthest removed in distance, they were done first. The sky was done entirely with the airbrush. The darker streaks are actually red, airpainted over a flat yellow tone. The lighter tones of the water were first airpainted in about the same color as the sky, and the darker streaks, which are blue, were dry-brushed over this.

FIG. 2. A frisket was placed over the entire painting and the mountain area exposed. A flat tone was airpainted towards the right where the mountains are more distant. The edges of the mountains against the sky were strengthened with darker color.

FIG. 3. The middle-value shadows of the mountains were painted opaquely with a handbrush directly over the airbrush areas; then, [FIG. 4] the deepest shadows were painted over these. The smoke from the volcanoes was airpainted with the AB model, using a small mask on the mountain peak. The flat middle value of the tree trunks was also handbrushed at this stage.

Fig. 4

Fig. 5

Fig. 6

FIG. 5. The foliage of the trees was broken down into two general areas — the light area of the foliage, and the dark, or shadow area. These were both laid in with flat opaque color, using the handbrush.

FIG. 6. The stems of the fronds were hand-brushed next; then the highlights and the strong, dark accents of the individual fronds brushed in. The tree trunks were completed in the same manner. The colors were used opaquely as they had to cover the colors of the background.

FIG. 10. A frisket was laid over the flower section and the entire area of the large flower exposed. A light tone of pink was airpainted over this area. Another frisket was placed over the previous one and a single petal exposed, enabling the modeling or shading of this petal to be accomplished without spilling over into the adjacent petals.

FIG. 11. Each petal was successively worked up in this particular manner, the darkest values being applied last.

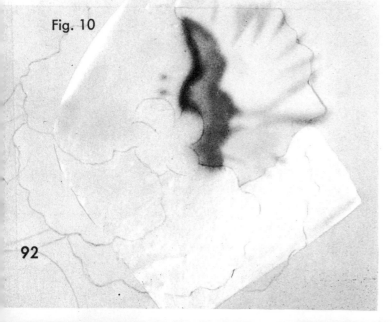

Fig. 10

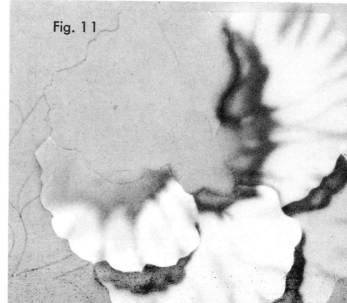

Fig. 11

Fig. 7

Fig. 8

Fig. 9

FIG. 7. After the figures were traced in position on the illustration, a frisket was placed over them and the flesh areas exposed. The flat body color was first airpainted, and then

[FIG. 8], the middle values of the shadows were filled in [FIG. 9]. The dark shadow accents were added with the handbrush, and the highlights were put in last. The clothes and vases were handled in the same manner.

FIG. 12. The frisket has been removed from the flower so that it can be shown before the addition of any line work. The leaves have been airpainted with a flat tone of green, and the one in the lower right has the beginning of the shading indicated. After the leaves were completely modeled, the veins were added with opaque light and dark color, using the handbrush, in very much the same manner as with the flowers.

FIG. 13. The frisket was removed. Again with the sable brush, the edges of the leaves and flowers were accented with opaque color, and any texture effects and details, such as in the center of the flower, were added.

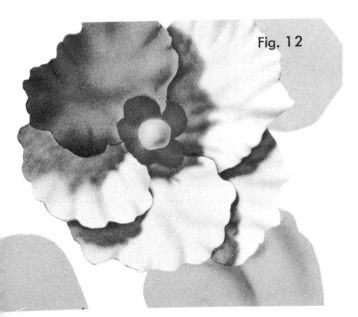

Fig. 12

Fig. 13

93

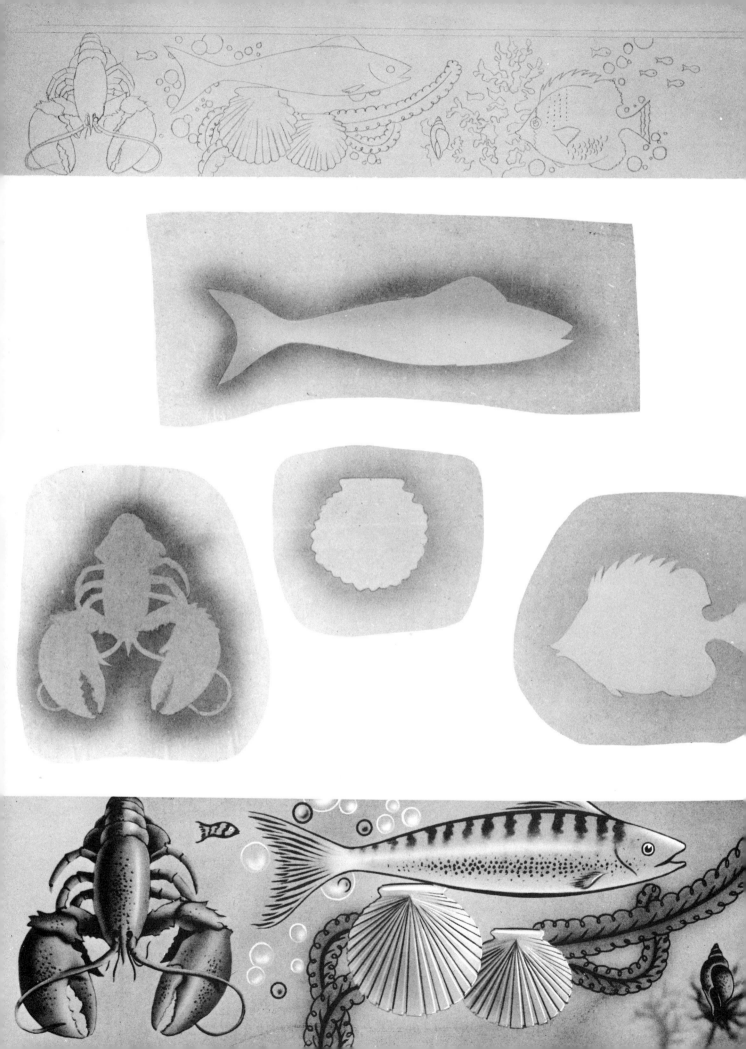

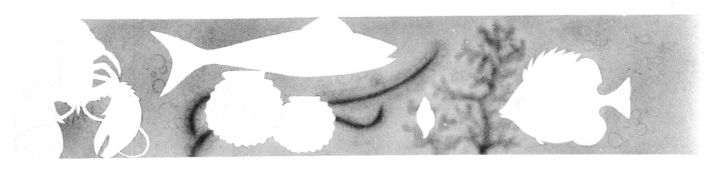

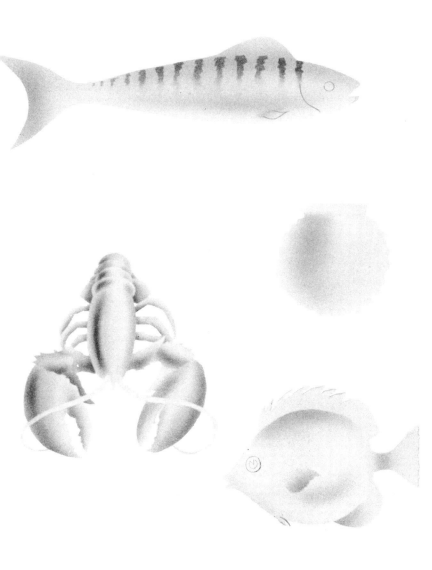

Design

The problems in this particular rendering do not differ much from those in the previous one. It is of value, however, to run through the procedure since this project differs from the last in subject matter.

An accurate color sketch was first made. The color was handled much more transparently than in the other project, so a clean, accurate pencil drawing was made. All objects were covered with a frisket, leaving the entire background, including the seaweed, exposed. The tone of the background was definitely required to be of a light middle value. Since the background tone and color affect the various objects placed against it, the background was airpainted first. The frisket was removed from the various objects. See above for this stage.

From here on, each object was frisketed separately and airpainted, first with the broad, basic colors, as shown at far left, and then with the shading colors, as shown on this page. With the exception of the lobster, all airbrush modeling was done only with the frisket shown. The lobster had to be covered with separate friskets for the body, the claws and the antennae, after the basic color had been applied. (Bear in mind that these are shown here as isolated objects merely for clarity of illustration. Actually, at this stage the background surrounded each of the objects in the original rendering.)

All line work was then added with a hand brush as shown in the finished illustration at the bottom. The circles for the bubbles were done in opaque water color, with a pen-compass.

Antonio Petruccelli

Antonio Petruccelli has been doing exquisitely conceived and executed air-brush illustrations for at least forty years, most of them for Life Magazine, Fortune, and Exxon's The Lamp. He works mostly with the Paasche AB air-brush, either totally freehand, as in the undersea illustration on the opposite page, or with frisket and handbrush, as on this and the lower half of 16b. Mr. Petruccelli executes the most minute detail without getting "fussy" or over-worked. His convincing atmospheric and environmental effects, his ability to delineate space, form and detail, while keeping all parts subordinant to the whole are partial keys to the success of his brilliant illustrations. The whole in the picture on the opposite page is shown on page 16c at about four fifths actual size of the original painting. Two details from his illustration on lower page 96b are shown at actual size of the original art on page 96c.

Antonio Petrucelli. The Lamp.

Antonio Petruccelli.
Life Magazine.

Maurello Studio

The illustration above is shown in black and white step-by-step procedure on page 90-93.

Right: Another of Mr. Petruccelli's combination of handbrush and freehand airbrush. The original is 16" x 7½". The ship at the lower right in the illustration is only 1⅛ inches long in the original.

Antonio Petruccelli. Life M.

A. Petruccelli

Maurello Studio

The illustration above is shown in black and white step-by-step procedure on page 90-93.

Right: Another of Mr. Petruccelli's combination of handbrush and freehand airbrush. The original is 16″ x 7½″. The ship at the lower right in the illustration is only 1⅛ inches long in the original.

Antonio Petruccelli. Life M...

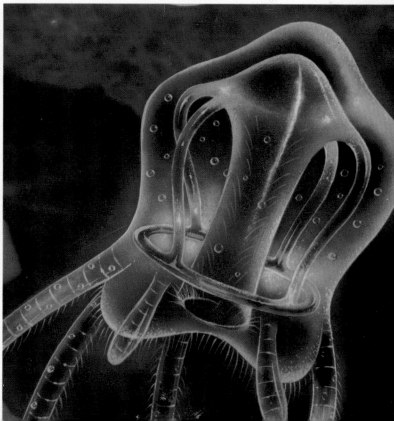

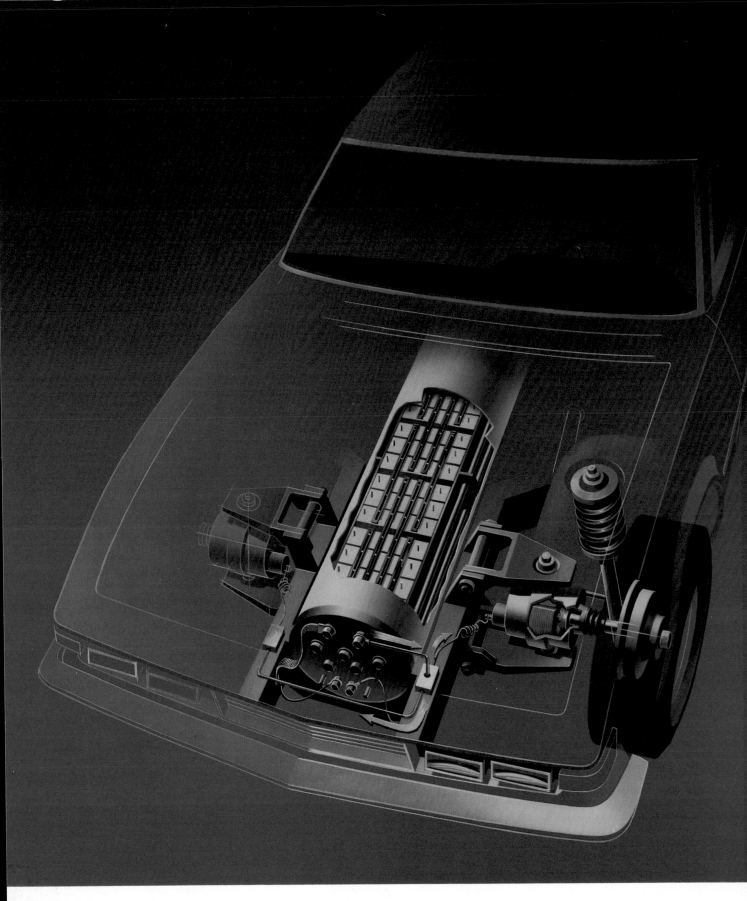

The airbrush is ideal for depicting
"phantom" views and cut-a-way sections.

Technical Illustration

Technical Illustration

Technical illustration is a rather broad term, applied generally to that type of art which illustrates, factually or symbolically, the construction, function or operation of a machine, physical phenomenon, industrial process, biological theory, etc. Such illustrations are used in instruction manuals and films, advertising material, textbooks, visual aids, displays, and exhibits, and various other media.

The art techniques used depend upon how the artwork will be reproduced or shown, the nature of the subject matter, the time and funds allowed, the scope of the instruction or campaign, and other factors. Airbrush has become particularly useful in this field of late because of its flexibility, its control, its shading and color blending characteristics. One of the most extensive applications is in the mechanical field, and for this reason I have chosen to show the step-by-step procedure for such an application in the Mechanical Illustration section beginning on page 116. This illustration was originally done for an instruction manual for the Walter Kidde Company. The original rendering was slightly larger than the reproduction shown here.

Botanical illustration. Royaledge Paper Co.

Medical Illustration—Watercolor illustration of newborn baby showing viscera. Original painted life size using drybrush technique and airbrush. Copyright R.J. Demarest, 1979.

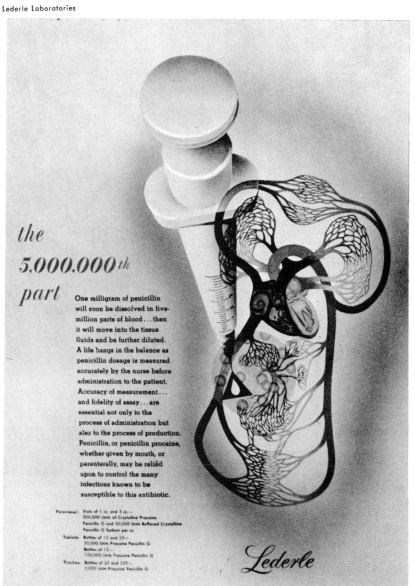

the
5.000.000th
part

One milligram of penicillin will soon be dissolved in five-million parts of blood...then it will move into the tissue fluids and be further diluted. A life hangs in the balance as penicillin dosage is measured accurately by the nurse before administration to the patient. Accuracy of measurement... and fidelity of assay...are essential not only to the process of administration but also to the process of production. Penicillin, or penicillin procaine, whether given by mouth, or parenterally, may be relied upon to control the many infections known to be susceptible to this antibiotic.

Parenteral: Vials of 1 cc. and 5 cc.—
300,000 Units of Crystalline Procaine
Penicillin G and 30,000 Units Buffered Crystalline
Penicillin G Sodium per cc.
Tablets: Bottles of 12 and 25—
50,000 Units Procaine Penicillin G
Bottles of 12
100,000 Units Procaine Penicillin G
Troches: Bottles of 25 and 250—
5,000 Units Procaine Penicillin G

Lederle

Medical illustration used for advertising purposes.

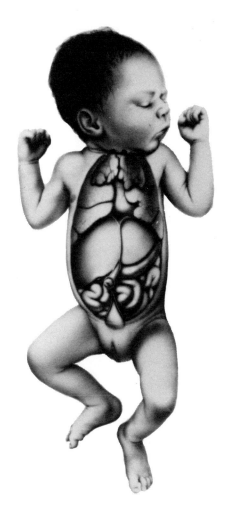

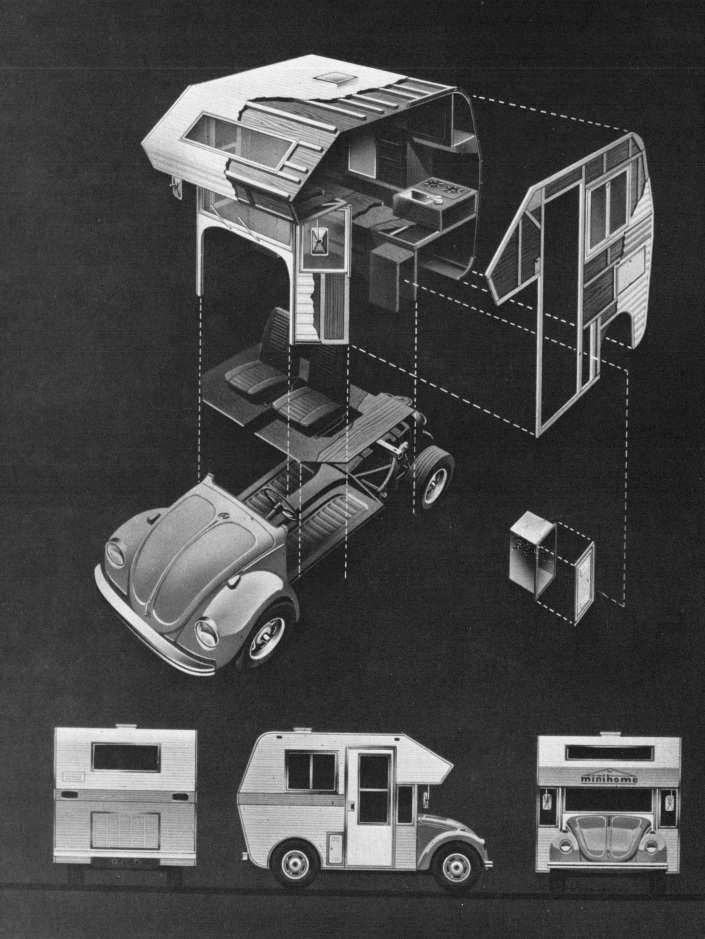

Van decoration by means of airbrush has become an extremely popular art form in the past few years. Scenics, murals, cartoons and other illustration subjects are applied directly to the metal or glass panels of the van or other vehicle body. Application is made either by means of friskets, stencils or freehand and some handbrush using acrylic enamels paint. The Paasche VL or VI airbrush and other industrial brushes are used. Purely geometric decorations are done with the Paasche Striper airbrush.

Using White Pigment on Black Ground

Working only with lampblack on a white ground necessitates working around the highlight areas. In other words, we make use of the white of the paper for our lights. With the black pigment we can only make the paper or the rendering darker than it is, but not lighter. After darkening an area with lampblack we can, however, use white tempera or poster paint in the airbrush and thus lighten the dark areas where necessary. In doing so we are changing our technique from a pure transparent one to a semi-opaque one. The caricature by Sam Berman on page 106 was done in this manner. A dark wash of gray tone (diluted lampblack) was first applied over the entire drawing with the handbrush; then white paint was used semi-opaquely in the airbrush to work up the renderings. Cut-out masks were used to control the shading and to build up the lights to the shapes and values desired.

Another effective technique is that of airpainting with white paint on a black paper background. Black drawing paper, Color-aid paper, or good mounting board may be used for this purpose. If the white paint is diluted thinly with water and applied lightly over the paper it will only lighten it slightly; heavier airpainting will lighten it still more, until a pure white tone is secured. The effective rendering by Mr. Leydenfrost on the opposite page was done in this manner.

Now we may go a step further and use both black and white pigments, alternately, on a *gray* background, as in the schematic on page 80. Thus we start with a middle value ground and make it both lighter and darker as desired. Our final step in this progression, aside from the use of full color, is to work with a full range of gray pigments, as well as black and white, as explained on page 75.

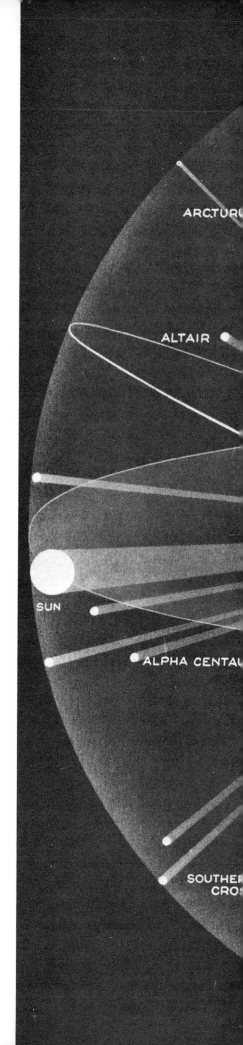

ARCTURU

ALTAIR

SUN

ALPHA CENTAU

SOUTHE
CRO

A. Leydenfrost
Life Magazine

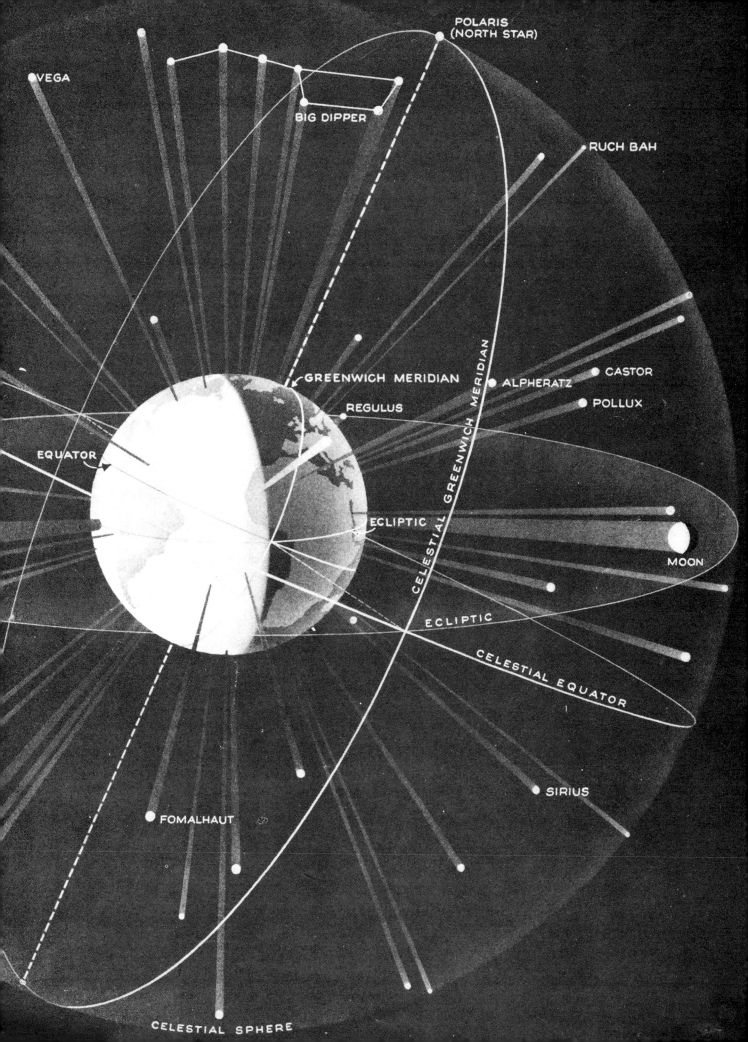

Portrait and Figure Rendering

Sam Berman

Portrait Rendering

The versatility of the airbrush is well indicated in these portrait renderings, ranging from the caricature at left, and the decorative stylization, below, to the realistic but delicate treatment of the woman's portrait, and the dramatic portrait of the man on the next page.

Jean Carlu

106

Varga
Jergen's Lotion

The technique used in the caricature by Mr. Berman is described on page 102. The portrait by Mr. Clark was airpainted in full color, and entirely freehand, using the Paasche AB Airbrush for the detail drawing. The original was very large, 20 by 23 inches, and done with opaque color, the darks for the most part having been applied first and the light colors built up over them.

Howell Clark

107

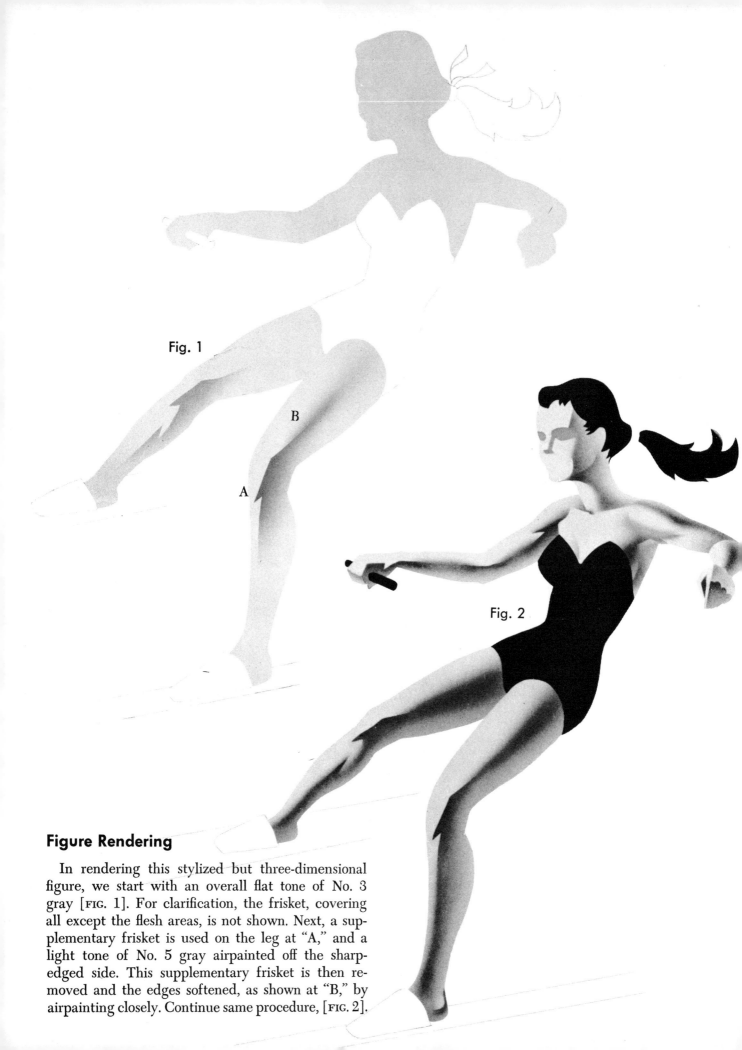

Fig. 1

A

B

Fig. 2

Figure Rendering

In rendering this stylized but three-dimensional figure, we start with an overall flat tone of No. 3 gray [FIG. 1]. For clarification, the frisket, covering all except the flesh areas, is not shown. Next, a supplementary frisket is used on the leg at "A," and a light tone of No. 5 gray airpainted off the sharp-edged side. This supplementary frisket is then removed and the edges softened, as shown at "B," by airpainting closely. Continue same procedure, [FIG. 2].

FIG. 3. All except the water area is covered with a frisket, and the flat tone of the water is airpainted with a No. 4 gray. [FIG. 4] The frisket is removed from the water spray area, and the spray is first air-brush stippled with white, then accented with hand-brush stipple after the skis are painted.

Fig. 3

Fig. 4

Otis Shepard
Wm. Wrigley Co., Jr.

Otis Shepard
Wm. Wrigley Co., Jr.

For many years Otis Shepard's advertisements for the Wm. P. Wrigley, Jr., Co. were probably the best known form of airbrush art in this country. Their individual and consistent style, long period of use and extensive distribution via car cards and billboards made them popular and familiar. Mr. Shepard did his original art the same size as the car cards, using the VL, which is the poster size airbrush, and employing friskets extensively. His general technique was to use a flat color with a shading color, often stippled or spattered, on top (see page 64a). Hand brush was kept to a minimum. He rarely used more than two colors over each other or closely intermingled. This is partly due to the manner in which the ads are reproduced . . . a method quite different from that ordinarily used. Instead of the usual four-color printing, a separate plate was made for each color in the original art, and instead of the plates being made photographically, the image for each color was applied to the plate manually, using liquid tusche in the airbrush and following Mr. Shepard's original faithfully. Thus the artwork is not broken up by a photo-engraving or lithographic screen, and each color can be matched in the printing because a separate plate is used to reproduce it. Having seen the program cover, page 64b, reproduced by this method as well as by the usual four-color process used here, it is evident that the former is certainly far more faithful to the original artwork.

Fine Arts Painting

In recent years the airbrush has been used by many fine artists as a painting tool, usually for applying acrylic paints to canvas. As in oil painting, cotton or linen canvas is fastened to a wooden stretcher frame. Acrylics can be conveniently used in the airbrush because, although they are soluble in water, they have the advantage of being waterproof and durable when dry, thus the framed painting does not require a glass covering as protection. If desired, they can be varnished, and are similar to oil painting in appearance as well as durability. Although, when applied with the handbrush (bristle, sable or nylon), acrylics do not blend or make color and tonal transitions as smoothly as oil, with the airbrush such effects are easily controlled and accomplished, as seen in William Wilson's "Resting," and in the convincing shadows of Paul Sarkisian's "Untitled," which looks like a montage, even when viewed in the original, but which is all acrylic paint on canvas.

Insofar as techniques of applying the paint or defining the forms with airbrush, either completely freehand airbrushing or complete masking or frisketing methods are used, or combinations of these, plus some handbrush. Masking and industrial tapes are often used, applied directly to the primed canvas or over previously acrylic painted areas, as neither the ground nor the painted surface are as delicate as the illustration board and watercolor paints used by the commercial artist. It should be noted that acrylics do not flow as easily as regular watercolors unless considerable diluted, and care must be taken not to allow the acrylics to dry in the airbrush, as, due to their waterproof quality when dry, they cannot be "soaked out" like watercolors. Depending upon the size and nature of the painting, the airbrush may be a large double action type such as the VL, or, where less control is required, large double action type such as the VL, or, where less control is required, or coarse spatter, the single action H brush. Both brushes will accept thicker paint, especially if air pressure is increased.

Though any size or style is possible, most current fine arts airbrush painting is done in large format (48"x60", for example), and photo realism seems to be the prevalent style, though the airbrush is applicable to stylized and abstract work, as well. Compare Chuck Close's small 6 inch by 9 inch "Self Portrait," done with airbrush "dots" within a grid patter, with David Mydans huge 60" x 90" hard-edged, semi-stylized "Romeo and Juliette," and "Jerry Ott's Study," with its smooth tonal transitions and soft photographic realism—a style somewhat different from his extremely photo-realistic painting, "Last Summer." In terms of airpainting style and techniques Audrey Flack's colorful realism differs considerable from Don Eddy's almost completely black and white linear pattern of glasses, shown in an almost actual size detail alongside the full painting.

Chuck Close. Self Portrait.
9" x 6". Louis K. Meisel Gallery.

David Mydans. "Romeo and Juliet." 60" x 90".

Jerry Ott. Study from Manson Tapes. 55" x 68". Louis Meisel Gallery.

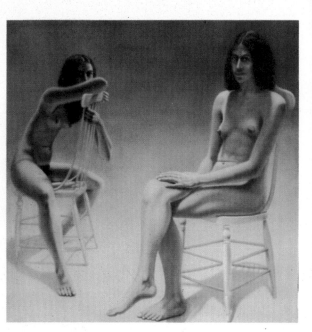

William Wilson. 60" x 60".

Audrey Flack. Dutch Still Life. 60" x 60". Louis K. Meisel Gallery.

Paul Sarkisian. Untitled. Acrylic on canvas. 78" x 112". Nancy Hoffman Gallery.

Don Eddy. G II. Acrylic on linen. 44″ x 40″. Nancy Hoffman Gallery.
Jerry Ott. Last Summer. 48″ x 60″. Louis K. Meisel Gallery.

Untitled. Thom O'Connor. Lithograph.

Airbrush image on old litho stone.

Silkscreen print. James Martin

Printmaking

The airbrush is of use in certain preparatory stages of printmaking such as lithography, etching, silkscreen, photogravure and gum bichromate printing. It can be used to spray liquid tusche, autographic ink, gum arabic, acid etch, and photoemulsion. In some cases the airbrush is used to draw the image, or certain stages of the image, in other cases it is used to apply an even coated ground or etch.

Airbrush can be used directly on the stone or plate, or it can be applied to acetate sheets where photographic emulsion is used to image a plate or screen. In such procedures the image on acetate is used like a positive photographic film, and light exposed through it to the emulsion on the plate or screen. (This information on the use of the airbrush is provided for those with a knowledge of printmaking procedures, and not intended as printmaking instructions per se.)

Depending upon the effect desired, as in the old lithograph stone, either a smooth "continuous tone" image is applied, or a fine to coarse stipple or spatter is used as in the O'Connor work; effects for which the airbrush is particularly suited. Generally the larger type airbrushes are used, such as the double action Paasche VL or the single action H model. Various tips on the latter model can be used to produce fine or coarse stipple. It is also possible to use the Paasche Air Eraser (page 20) with fine pumice powder to reduce or eradicate an area of tusche that has been applied to a metal plate or stone. In addition to stipple and spatter, varied texture and pattern effects can be obtained by laying down, on the plate or acetate, such materials as rice, sand, chicken wire, wire mesh, lace, etc., spraying liquid tusche into the air over the materials, and letting it gently settle down on them, if they are likely to be disturbed by direct action of the spray.

An example of airbrush procedure as applied in the use of spatter and stipple on acetate for exposing photographically an image to a screen for screen printing.

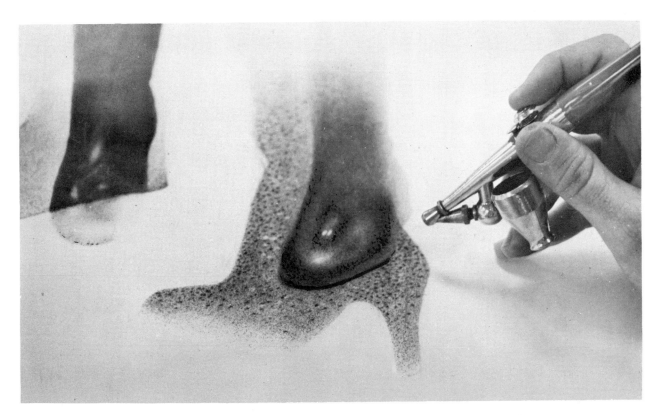

Mechanical Illustration

Mechanical illustration involves the rendering of machinery or related equipment, either as a complete object, showing only its external view or more often showing at least a partial internal view or complete internal structure or function. Usually a cut-a-way section is involved "slicing off one-fourth of the object as on page 117. The purpose may be only to identify parts in their proper position.

Such renderings can be drawn either from "orthographic" projections—the front side top and bottom views of the subject with the artist using such reference to make a perspective drawing or an isometric drawing. In the latter case the drawing is built on a vertical axis with horizontals going out from this at 30° or one side and 60° on the other and all measurements actual size. This gives a somewhat oversized view of the object with some distortion but is simpler than true perspective.

Often a straight front view is used in the illustration on page 116 as this is modeled or shaded to make it look 3-dimensional. A cut-away section might be shown to reveal further structure. It is easier to work with a water proof ink outline and shade this with lamp black, used transparently, but often mechanical renderings are done completely with opaque color.

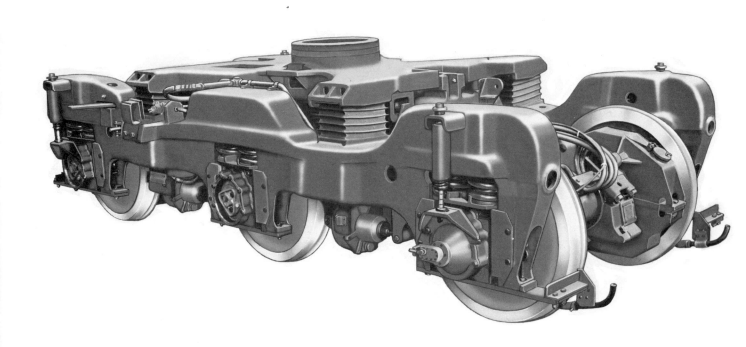

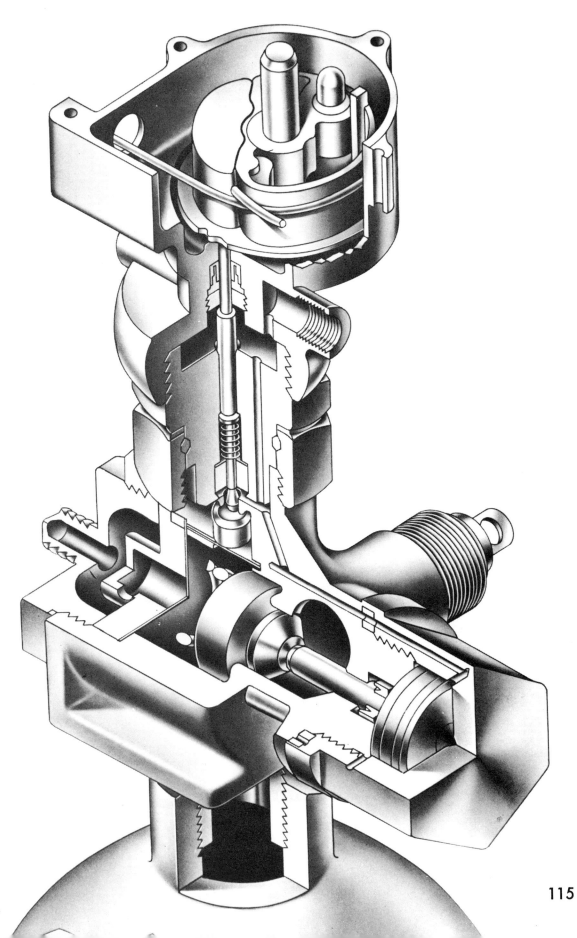

Valve Rendering

This particular project is typical of the pen-line transparent color illustration used in technical and instruction manuals. To a considerable extent this follows the formula for shading used in the rendering of the cube, cylinder and sphere earlier in the book. In this particular instance an isometric drawing (rather than a perspective drawing) was made from the blueprints of the valve. The airbrush artist is not always required to work out this particular phase of the drawing, as he sometimes receives either a pencil tracing or an inked outline on which to work. A sheet of tracing paper placed over the outline drawing can be used to make a preliminary rough indication of the shading in pencil. The outline drawing was traced on a sheet of hot-pressed illustration board and inked. The ruling pen can be used throughout, but the Wrico pen, as explained on page 66, is preferable, especially for indicating the threads and other curved parts, as well as assuring uniform thickness of all lines throughout the entire drawing.

If the ink drawing has to be corrected in spots, or is not quite as clean-cut and satisfactory as required, it is advisable to touch up with opaque white wherever necessary. However, since this white paint would affect the transparent black during airpainting, it is advisable to get a glossy negative photostat of the drawing, retouch further on that in ink and white paint, and then have a final positive glossy photostat, exactly the same size as the rendering, made from this. Be certain that the stat is properly fixed and washed by the stat maker. A photographic print, instead of the stat, can also be used. The positive stat should be mounted on heavy board either with rubber cement or by the dry mounting process. Be careful not to soil the surface of the stat when mounting, as any irregularities in the surface of the paper will affect the smoothness of the transparent wash. One advantage of doing the rendering on the photostat is that incorrect shading can be wiped away with moist cotton as explained on page 139.

Since the shading is predetermined, one can start almost anywhere; this one was done from the top down in order not to disturb any completed areas. Only a small frisket was placed over the drawing as only a small area was being worked on. More than one section can be exposed at one time if they are not adjacent to each other. Several areas were shaded using this one frisket, supplemented with masks.

The previous frisket was removed and another placed over the area and cut out as indicated by the white sections. Since the frisket now covers the areas that were airpainted in the previous stage, this shading is subdued, but is distinguishable.

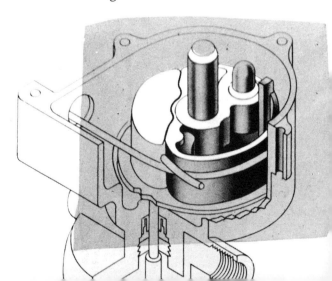

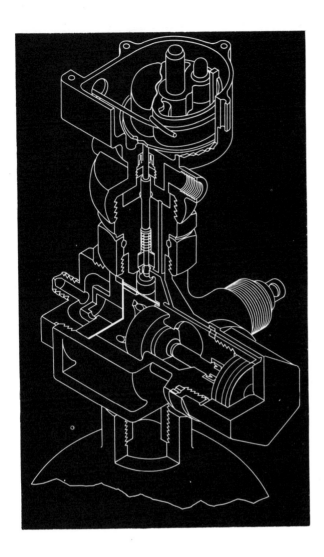

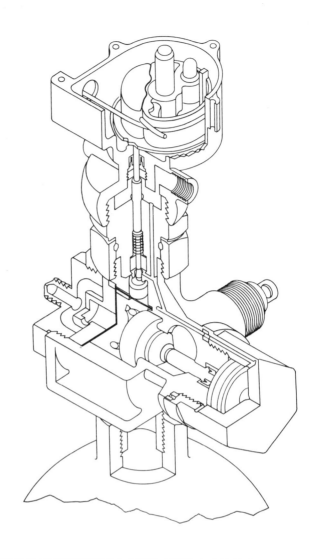

The side and bottom planes of the housing form a fillet or soft edge, which would catch the light. Since opaque color was not being used in this particular rendering, it was necessary to leave this light area and work around it. This was accomplished by making two strokes with the AB airbrush, as shown, and working outwards from these two lines.

The completion of the entire section is shown. As all frisket cutting was done on the black outline it might be necessary to touch up this outline with black paint.

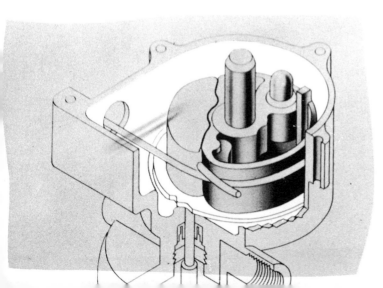

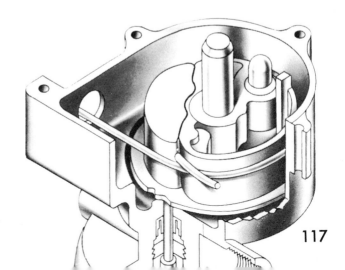

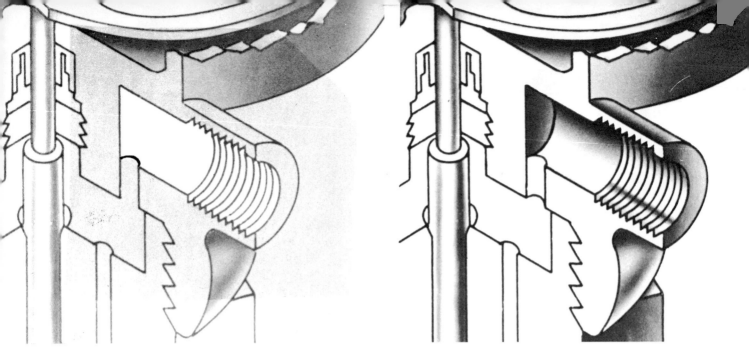

Inside Threads: For the sake of clarity, this section is shown larger than the actual size of the rendering. The area to be shaded has been exposed. There are various ways of rendering thread forms but the particular one used here follows our cylinder shading formula. This can be more clearly seen on the outside threads below.

The shading of the major shape of the cylinder was done first. Since this is an inside view of the cylinder form, the top is in shadow and the bottom is light.

Outside Threads: A frisket was placed over this section and the entire group of threads exposed. As in the outside cylinder form, a heavy shadow was airpainted at the bottom and a lighter one at the top, leaving reflected lights along the edges.

The previous frisket was removed and replaced with a new one. By cutting the frisket carefully along the black line, only the first thread was exposed, then a narrow shadow was airpainted off the edge of the frisket. The second thread was exposed and the same procedure followed.

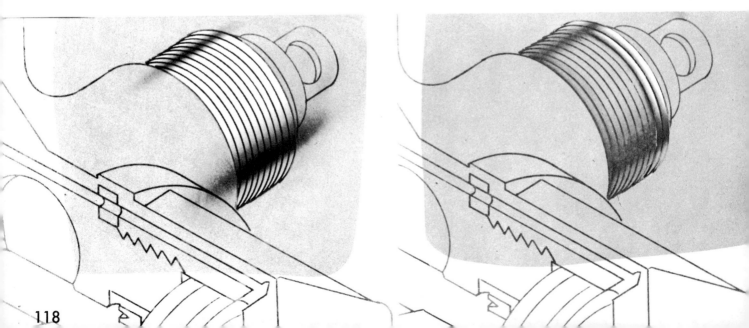

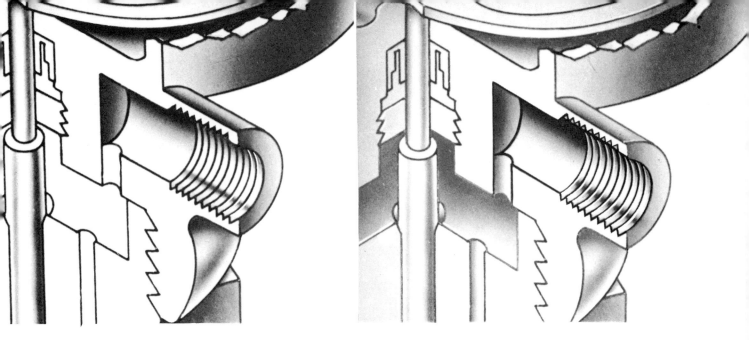

Each of the individual threads was separated by a white highlight line drawn freehand with the sable brush and opaque white (permissible for linework).

At the top section of the cylinder, which is in heavy shadow, this white would be a little too strong, so it was toned down by airpainting a little transparent black over it.

Each thread was airpainted until the entire section was completed. With the handbrush and opaque white, each thread was highlighted carefully, alongside the black ink line. The background frisket was left on while doing this. After the highlighting was completed, a few strokes of transparent black were airpainted over these highlight lines to subdue them slightly in the shadow areas.

The frisket was removed and any necessary touching up done along the edges.

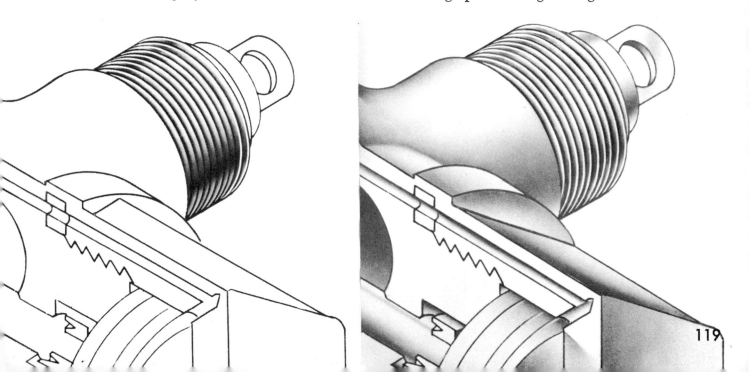

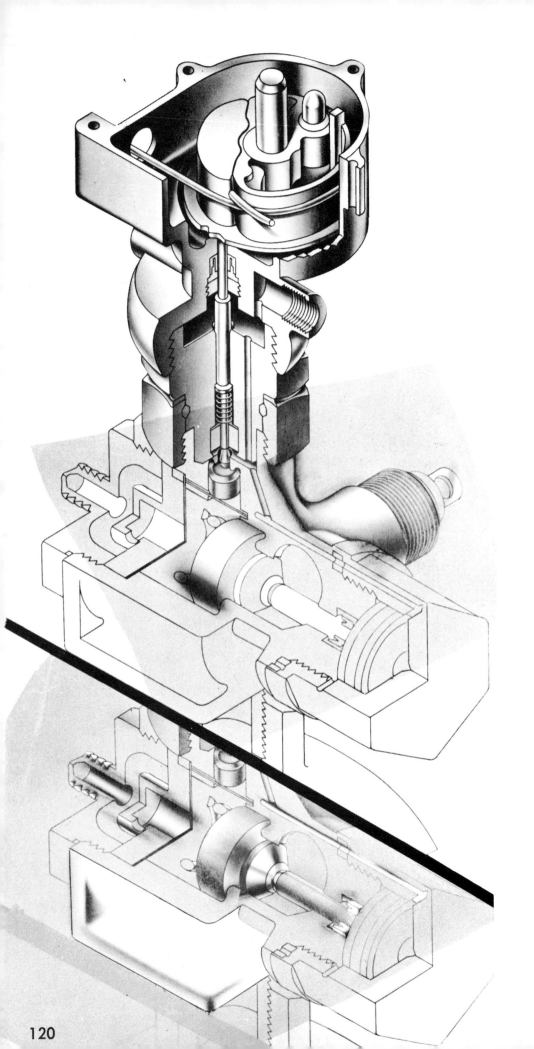

The vertical section of the valve has been rendered. Since it was required that one face of the cut-away section remain white, no shading was applied to this particular face except where channels and other hollow areas occur.

Moving down to the next area, the frisket is shown with several sections cut out, ready for airpainting. As before, these sections were staggered so that some frisket was left in between, and each was shaded individually.

The previous frisket has been replaced by a new one over the same area, and the remaining sections exposed and airpainted. Also, in this stage, the outside body of the valve has been started. Since this consists of all soft edges, no masks were used within the frisketed section. The airpainting shown here was done freehand and served mainly to define the edges of the various planes.

The rendering is shown carried slightly further. The reflected lights have been left by airpainting on either side of them, as was done previously on the top section of the valve.

The modeling was completed and a cast shadow added at the left of the bottom plane. A mask was used for this shadow.

The frisket has been removed from the entire area, showing the illustration before any highlight lines and additional dark lines were added. Referring to the finished illustration, you will note where these lines have been placed, and what further airpainting was done.

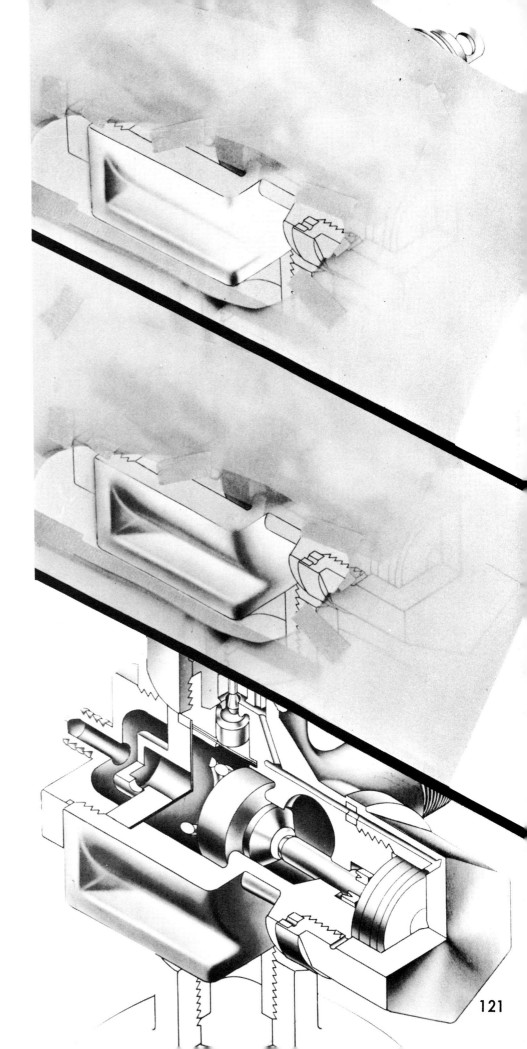

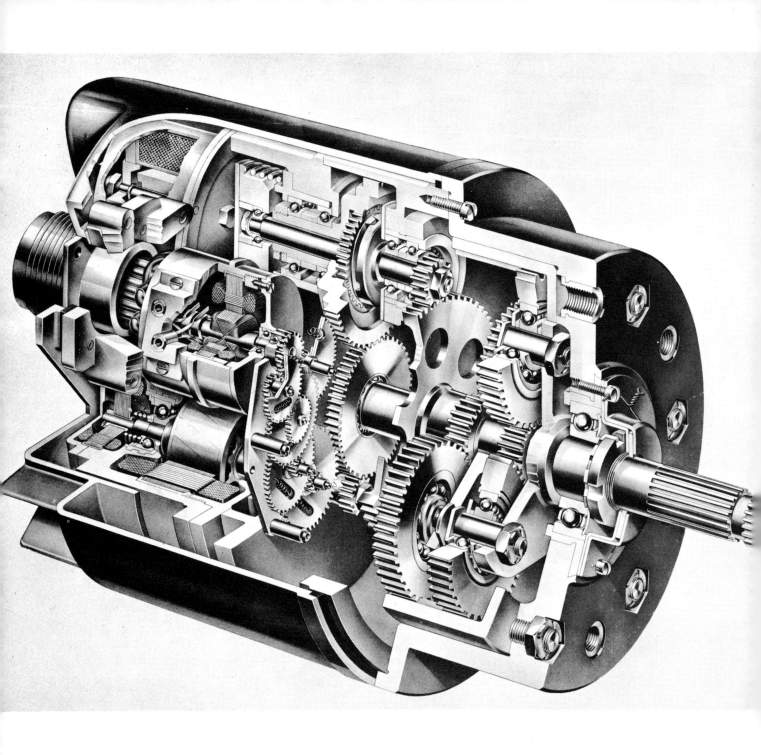

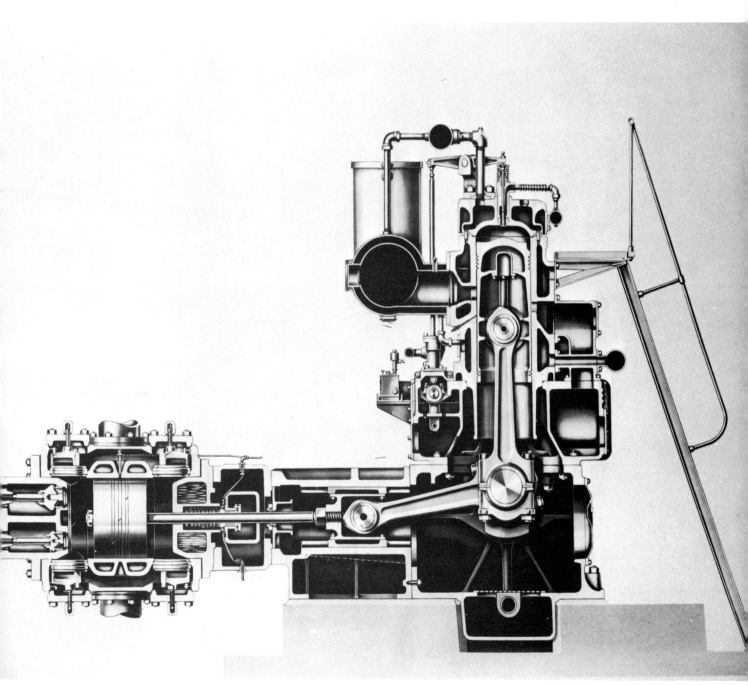

123

Architectural Rendering

Architectural Rendering

A finished architectural rendering is shown above. This was done with opaque color, although the color was used semi-transparently in certain areas such as the reflections on the windows. The pencil line drawing on tracing paper (insert) was provided by the architect. This was traced on kid-finish illustration board and a shaded overlay made on tracing paper in pencil as a rough guide before rendering.

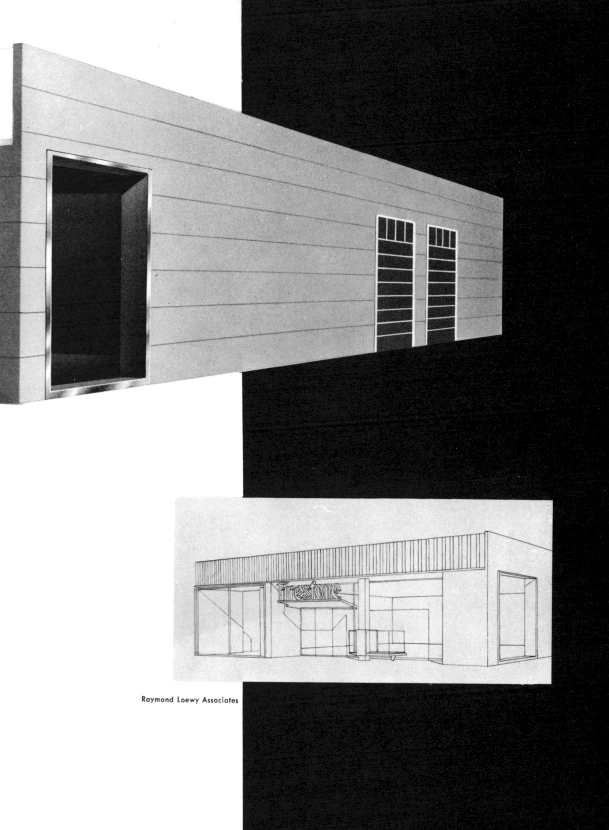

Raymond Loewy Associates

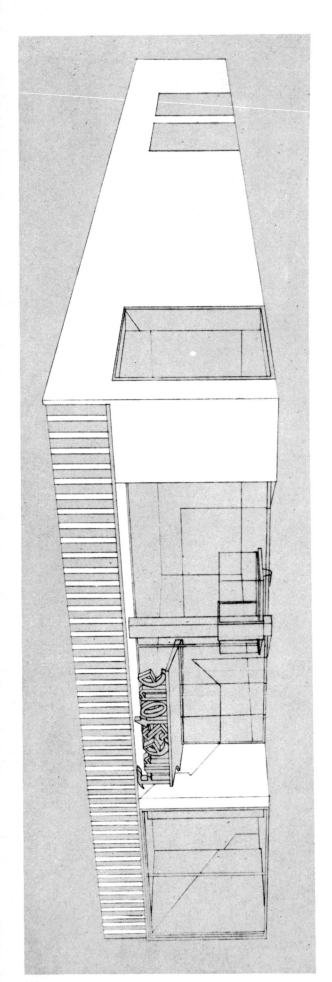

Working with the broadest areas first, the entire front and side walls of the building were exposed.

A flat tone of No. 2 gray was airpainted over the entire area. The stripes along the top front of the building were included in this shading.

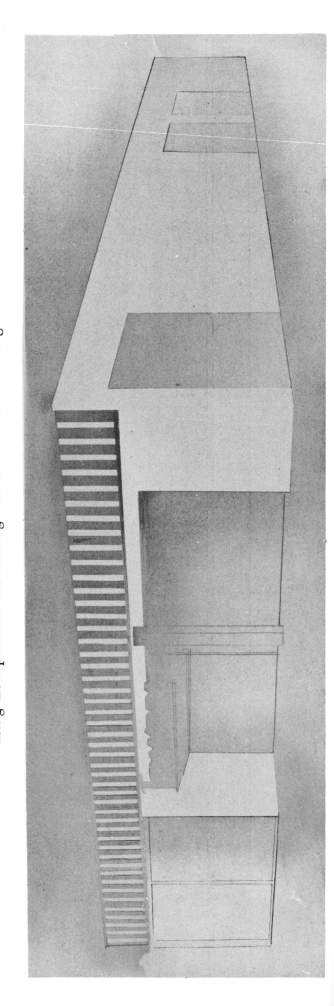

128

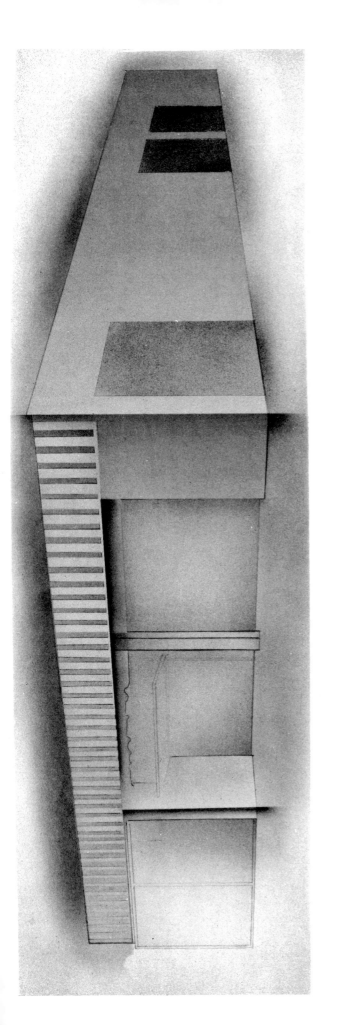

Each section was shaded as shown, using a No. 5 gray, with paper masks where necessary, as at the near corner of the building. To accent light and shadow planes, a No. 1 gray was airbrushed over the light areas just adjacent to the strongest darks, as on the right plane of the near corner of the building.

With the frisket removed, this illustration shows what has been done up to this point.

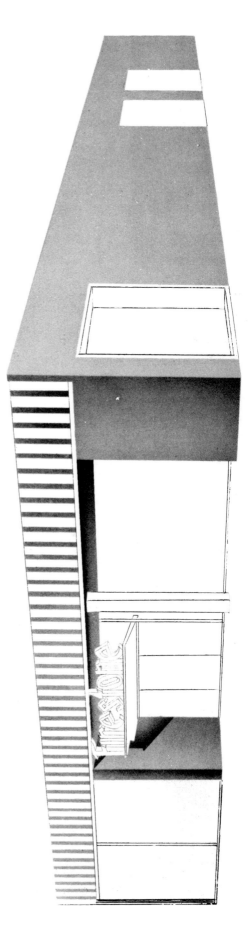

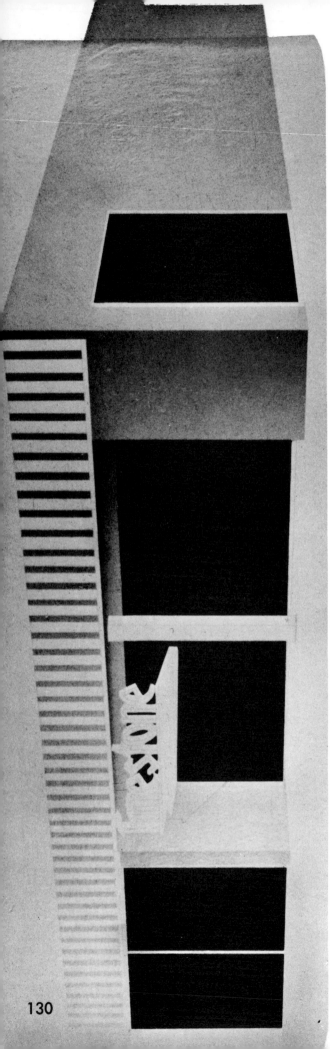

A new frisket was used, the entire window areas exposed and a solid black tone airpainted over them. The inside ceiling was covered with a supplementary frisket as this ceiling was to remain solid black. White pigment, used semi-transparently, was lightly airpainted over all the remaining window area, representing the major reflection. On top of this, additional reflections were later built up in several stages with white pigment using masks where necessary (as shown prematurely, for the sake of clarity, in the left window of the building).

It was necessary to trace the boundaries of these reflections on the black window area, using white chalk on the back of the tracing paper, instead of pencil, to make the transfer. The reflections are shown at a semi-completed stage. Illustration below shows the completion of the window area with the frisket removed. Now the solid black of the ceiling, where the supplementary frisket was put on previously, can be more clearly seen.

The outside showcase was traced on the window area, a frisket placed over this, and the entire glass area of the case exposed. Using paper masks, this was worked up with lampblack and opaque white. The frame of the showcase was airpainted and all linework added.

A frisket was placed over the lettering and the shadow side of the lettering exposed. Solid black was airpainted in these shadow areas. Applying masks where necessary, No. 3 gray was used to separate the different planes, as can be seen in the last letter. Leaving the same frisket on, the front planes of the letters were exposed and a little transparent black used to flash the front faces of the letters. (Since the shadow planes are much darker, any spill-over would not be visible.) This is shown in the final step, with the frisket removed and shadow and highlight lines added.

A new frisket was placed over the entire window areas and all the metal molding exposed. This was flashed with diagonal streaks of black and white.

After airpainting the molding, the frisket was removed and shown here before any linework was added.

Joseph Binder
Roy S. Durstine, Inc.
Seagram Distillers, Inc.

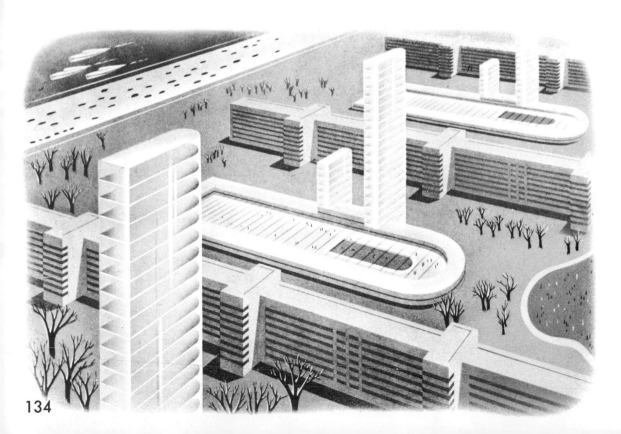

Photo Retouching

Photo Retouching

Photographs are retouched for various reasons. In the majority of cases, retouching is done in order to secure good reproduction qualities when the photograph is to be reproduced in printed form, as in a newspaper, magazine, etc. Next in importance is the necessity to present the product or subject photographed to best advantage, especially for advertising purposes. Again, the limitations of the camera or the circumstances under which the photograph was taken may have to be compensated for by retouching. Special effects such as fading out the image around the edge (vignette) or elimination of the background, combining part of one photograph with another, emphasizing only certain portions of a photograph, etc., are achieved through retouching. Restoration of old photos is a field in itself. For the most part, retouching of the types mentioned is done with the airbrush and handbrush on the positive print. This retouched photo is used by the publication, or the platemaker if it is to be used in printed form, or it is copied and additional photographic prints made if desired. Naturally the retouching that was on the original print will appear in the copies.

Photo retouching is a subject broad and important enough to require another volume. However, the airbrush methods presented in this book apply to retouching as well, and have to be mastered first. Enough information is given here to show what can be done and to indicate the general method of approach to working on photos as compared to airbrush painting or rendering.

Preparation of Photo: Most photographs which are to be retouched are of glossy, single weight stock. It is advisable to mount the photograph on a sheet of mounting or cheap illustration board at least two inches wider than the photograph on all sides, to allow for handling. The photograph can be rubber-cement mounted, the cement being applied to the back of the photograph and also to the face of the mounting board. Both should be allowed to dry a few minutes before being put together. Another method is to use photographic dry mounting tissue, made by Eastman Kodak Company. For this purpose an electrically heated dry mounting press or an electric iron is required.

After being mounted, the photograph should be rubbed down with a small wad of cotton dipped in talcum powder or moistened with saliva. Though seemingly unsanitary, the latter method is handy and effective, but care must be exercised not to wipe back and forth over the same area, or the moist cotton will stick. Photos are rubbed down in this manner before retouching to remove any grease spots caused by handling, and to provide a slight "tooth" to the surface so that the paint will adhere evenly. Keep a clean sheet of tracing paper or scrap paper beneath the hand when working on the photo after it has been cleaned. Protect the photo with an overlay of paper after it has been retouched, letting the paper adhere only along the top edge.

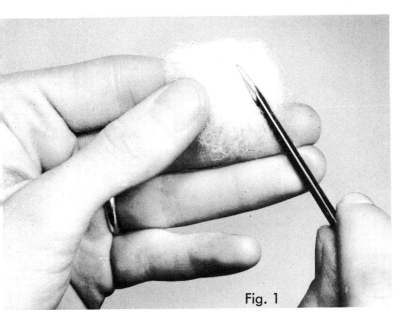

Fig. 1

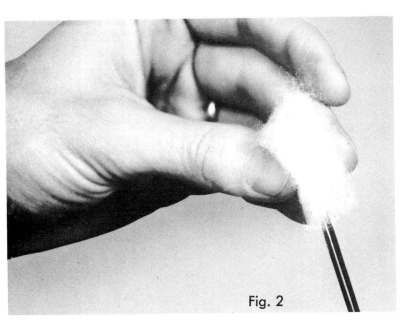

Fig. 2

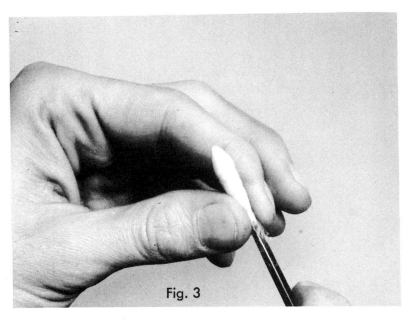

Fig. 3

Wipe-A-Way

Watercolor or dyes are applied to a photograph by means of the airbrush and sable brush, just as on illustration board or paper, with one additional advantage: that watercolor, transparent or opaque, can be easily wiped off the photo with a small wad of cotton as illustrated below. Therefore, it is not always necessary to use a mask or frisket. Also, mistakes can thus be corrected.

The cotton for wiping away should be of the long strand type, such as sterilized medical cotton [FIG. 1]. A small wad of the cotton is flattened and the wooden end of a brush placed in the center. The paint has been shaved from the brush end, shaping it to a point to facilitate adherence, and to control the size of the wad.

FIG. 2. The cotton is "folded" to envelop the brush end. While in this position the brush is twirled slowly with the right hand, rolling the cotton around the brush [FIG. 3]. While this is being done, the left thumb and forefinger should gradually move down to the base of the cotton, stretching and tightening it [FIG. 4]. The cotton may now be moistened in the mouth, or its tip lightly dampened in clean water, and so used to wipe away any watercolor which has been spilled over the image during airpainting. See bottom illustration. A clean sharp edge can be wiped away by this method, but it is advisable to use a mask or frisket where heavy airpainting or intricate or mechanically correct areas are to be rendered.

Fig. 4

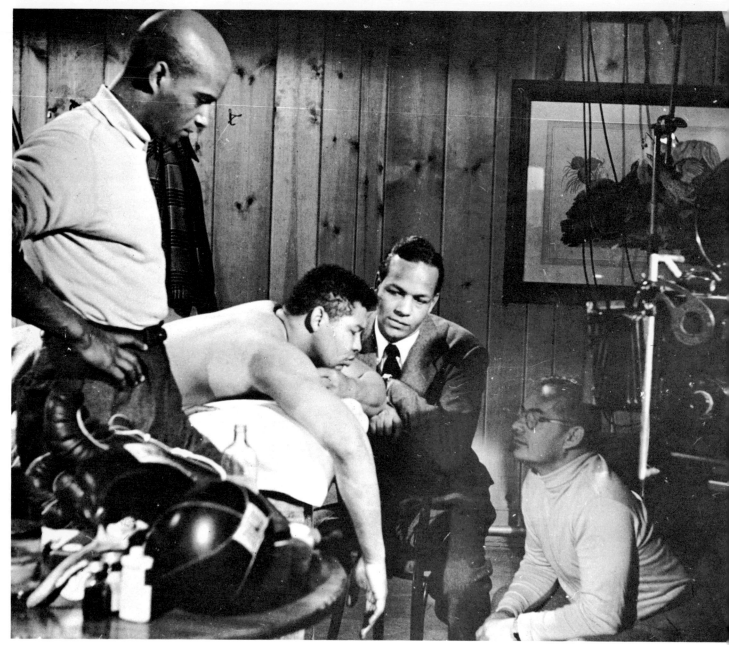

Newspaper Retouching

Since the coarse screen of the newspaper and the type of paper used do not hold the rather subtle distinctions of tones or fine lines that may appear in a photograph, retouching for newspaper reproduction entails a bolder and more definite treatment. As an example of the tone problem, if the hair on the cameraman in the above photo were just slightly darker than the wall behind him the distinction would be visible to the eye in the original photo, but the tones would be indistinguishable in the newspaper reproduction, unless exaggerated. One could either make the wall lighter or the hair darker. Note the difference in the same section of the photo on the opposite page, which has been retouched. Bringing out an object in this manner is known as "separation," and, in general, is what one should accomplish before anything else if the time or expense allotted to the job limits the work to be done. Separation by tonal differences, rather than by drawing

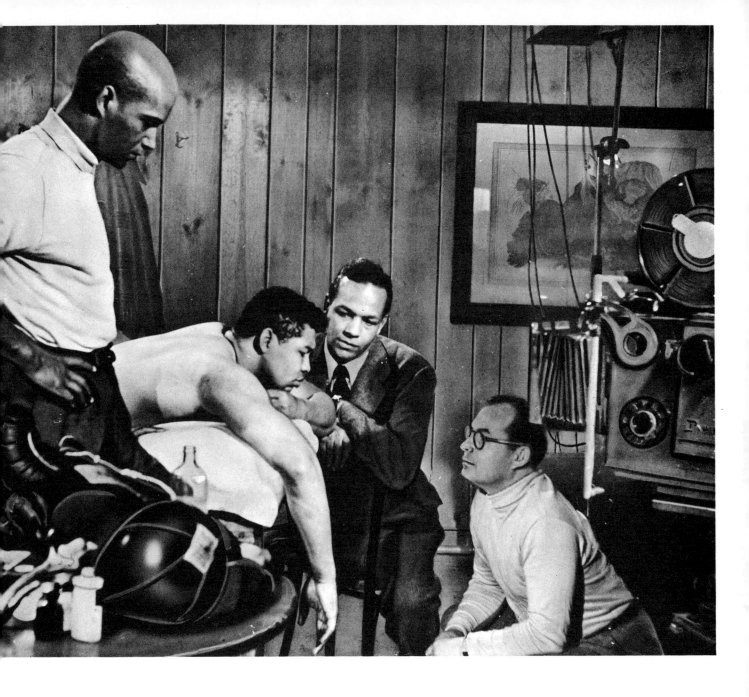

harsh outlines is to be preferred. The latter looks artificial, except where the subject matter calls for such line treatment, as in the motion picture camera in this photograph, or where extreme reduction of the image necessitates such treatment. Note how, by comparing the "before" and "after" photos, separation and clarity were accomplished. The jacket on the wall behind the standing figure was "toned down," or lightened so that it would not confuse the outline of the man's face or assume too much importance. The slightly out-of-focus objects in the lower left corner were separated from each other, and from the objects surrounding them, and more clearly defined by the use of linework. "Joe Louis'" arm was darkened to stand out against the white sheet, the chair in the center emphasized, the image in the picture on the wall toned down so that the equipment in front of it would stand out.

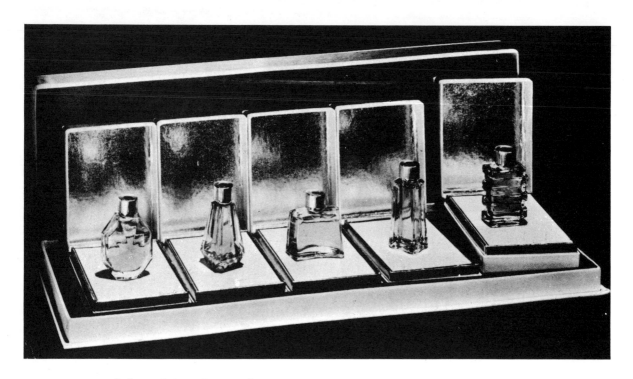

Advertising Retouching

This photograph was used primarily to advertise a newly designed package introducing a "set" of Ciro Perfumes. Since the package was still at the production stage at the time the advertising was being prepared, the photograph was made from a "dummy" package not quite as perfectly made as the manufactured package. Aside from correcting such defects it was necessary to do any shading and outlining required to bring out the form and local color of the various parts; to provide adequate separation between background and package, and between the various units; to eliminate undesirable images in the bottles, without losing the "glassy" look, and to assure good reproduction.

Ciro Parfums, Larry Gumbiner Advertising Agency

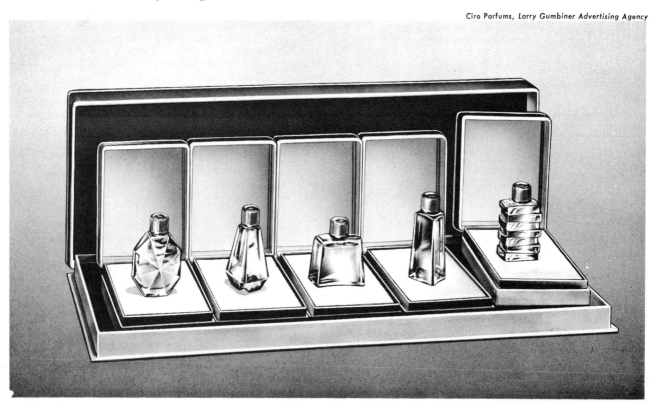

Corrective Retouching

Quite often the retouch artist is called upon to eliminate, replace or alter important portions of a photograph.

Let's consider a specific case. The above photograph was to be used as a cover for *American Druggist* magazine. The plant in front of the arm, the pen and the ashtray were considered objectionable, so they had to be removed. Unless otherwise requested, the logical thing to do when removing an object is to restore whatever it conceals: in this case the woman's arm, the desk top and blotter. The pen was airpainted out first, since this could be done without a frisket. Each value of the dress behind the pen was matched, working quite close so that the area covered would be kept to a minimum. A frisket was placed over the arm and its surrounding area. The outline of the missing portion of the arm was drawn in pencil directly on this frisket and the hand and arm area exposed. A retouch gray which matched the middle value of the arm was used to airbrush out the leaves; then highlight and shadow were airpainted, the latter semi-transparently. Only that portion of the arm and hand requiring coverage was airpainted. (If, when using a light gray over a dark image such as this, the paint takes on a cold, bluish tone which is out of key with the rest of the photograph, add a little yellow ochre water color to the light gray.)

The frisket was removed and replaced with one covering the desk area. The desk top was exposed; the ashtray and flower-pot were airpainted out, matching local values with the retouch grays; a little drybrush was used to restore the wood-grain effect, and a little color airpainted over this semi-transparently to subdue the drybrush. Retaining the same frisket, the blotter area was exposed, and airpainted, a mask shielding the desk. The shadow of the arm on the blotter was then airpainted.

American Druggist Magazine

143

Mechanical Retouching

This project represents a semi-mechanical subject to be "slicked-up" for catalogue reproduction, with corrective changes to be made in the counter. The unit was photographed at the factory on a dummy wooden counter. It was necessary to change this to a metal counter and alter the perspective of the counter slightly to allow the addition of a syrup container at the near end.

FIG. 1. Comparing the original photo with the retouched photo on the opposite page it will be noted that the "slicking-up" phase of the work consisted of eliminating irregular highlights on the body of the unit, defining the form more clearly by shading, thus separating front, side and top planes, lightening and sharpening the lettering, shading and defining the black rubber gaskets, lightening the shadow cast by the body on the metal base of the unit, defining planes and edges of the metal base, and "flashing" the metal of the valve handle. Each of these operations, performed in the order mentioned, involved frisketing each area consecutively as it was retouched. Lettering and linework, of course did not require friskets.

FIG. 2. This shows the beginning stage of the shading on the body of the unit. For clarity, the frisket is not shown here, but at this stage everything would be covered by the frisket, except the two areas being airpainted — the top cover of the unit and the body of the unit including the lettering. It will be noted that the shading has been allowed to fall on the beginning letters of "Coca-Cola" and "ice cold." This will be cleaned out with a wet cotton swab as shown on page 139. The same would apply to any spill-over on the white circular medallion on the left side of the unit. Now the high-lights are airpainted and the projecting unit of the medallion shaded. The frisket is removed, replaced by a new one and the rubber gaskets exposed and retouched. Procedure is continued as outlined above.

The beginning stage of the corrective work on the counter is also shown in this photo. The outline of the new counter has been drawn with hand-brush directly over the old one with opaque white. From here on, the old counter is ignored and the new outline used as the basis for rendering the metal one.

Cleaning and Maintenance

Cleaning and Maintenance

Many airbrush users do not clean or maintain their airbrushes beyond the cursory flushing out after use. Since one's artwork is directly dependent upon proper — I might almost say "perfect" — functioning of the airbrush, it would be well to spend an hour learning to provide adequate care and maintenance. The Paasche V, V Jr., and VL Airbrushes are comparatively easy to care for and any cause of improper functioning can usually be determined. It is necessary first to know the various parts of the brush and their functions. The chart on the opposite page shows the parts of the airbrush in their relative, or "exploded view," positions, with the identifying name of each part. When ordering parts, it is necessary to give the *part number,* which is listed on the parts sheet provided with the airbrush. On pages 150-151 the gradual disassembly of the airbrush is shown. Inadequate functioning of the brush is generally due to: (1.) improper adjustment of parts, such as not having the needle all the way in and screwed in securely; (2.) dirty, rusted or clogged airbrush, due to inadequate cleaning or abuse; (3.) injury to a part, such as a bent needle or split tip. All such likely difficulties and their corrections are explained and illustrated in the following pages. Read everything first and check things systematically; in actual practice, don't take the whole brush apart only to learn that your trouble was due to the fact that the color cup was clogged with thick paint.

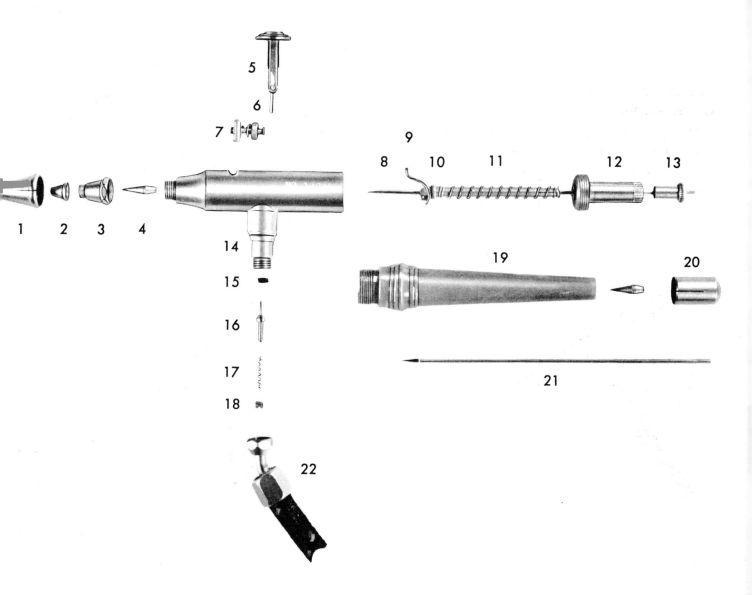

TYPE V1, VL, and V Jr. PAASCHE AIRBRUSH ASSEMBLY

1. Protecting Cap
2. Aircap
3. Centering Sleeve
4. Tip
5. Finger Lever
6. Finger Lever Piston
7. Line Adjustment Assembly
8. Needle
9. Rocker
10. Needle Support
11. Spring

12. Action Adjusting Sleeve
13. Needle Locknut
14. Valve Casing
15. Valve Washer
16. Valve Plunger
17. Valve Spring
18. Valve Nut
19. Handle
20. Rear Cap
21. Reamer
22. Hose Coupling Assembly

Construction and Functions of the Airbrush

While it is not necessary to take the brush completely apart before using, it is advisable to have some knowledge of its construction and the functioning of the various parts for future cleaning, and adjustment. Unscrew the action adjusting sleeve.

Remove the entire assembly from the brush. A spring is located between the rocker and the adjusting sleeve. By screwing the adjusting sleeve further into the airbrush shell, tension is increased on this spring and correspondingly increased on the finger lever when pulling back. If it is screwed too far, it interferes with the movement of the finger lever. If it is not screwed in far enough, it does not return to its position rapidly enough.

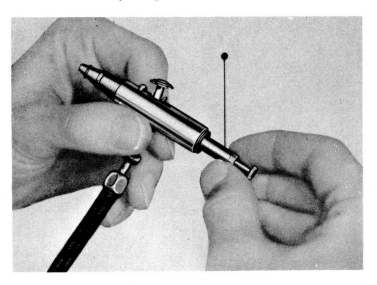

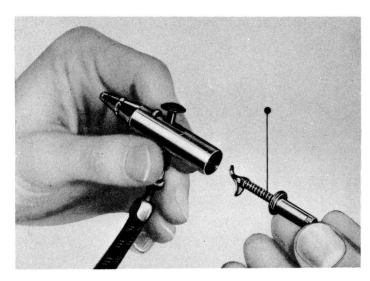

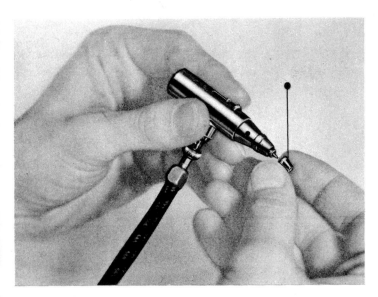

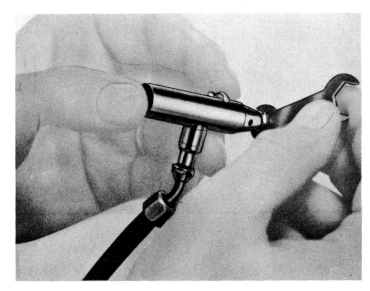

The air cap can be removed from the front end of the brush by hand, exposing a small portion of the tip.

The head of the brush must be removed by means of the wrench. When replacing the head, be sure that it is screwed on firmly, as air will leak out of this joint if it is not tightened completely.

The finger lever can be removed by pulling it out, revealing the lever pivot attached to the base of the trigger. When reinserting, be sure that this lever pivot is in an upright position and slides down into the valve casing.

By examining the back of the finger lever, you will note that there is a channel through it. The finger lever cannot be removed from the brush until the needle is pulled back beyond this point. If the needle, when being gently inserted, does not go all the way forward, simply pull it back slightly and check the finger lever to see if it is seated properly.

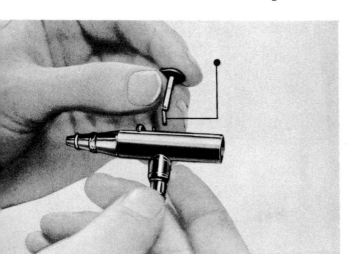

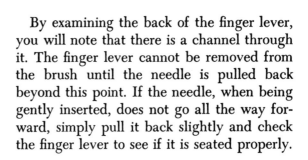

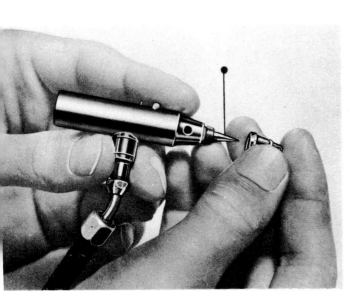

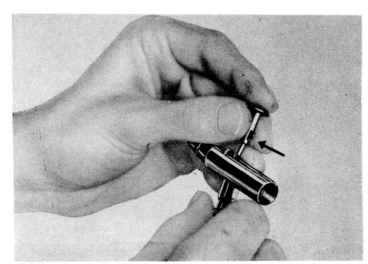

Removal of the head now exposes the tip, which is seated firmly in the airbrush.

Very gently but firmly wiggle the tip out of its place with the fingers. When clogged, the tip can be cleaned as indicated on page 153. When injured, the tip can be replaced by a new one. It is not necessary to force the tip back into place, as the pressure exerted by the replacement of the head will seat it firmly. To put the brush together again, merely reverse the procedure outlined here.

Cleaning and Care of the Brush

FIG. 1. When through airpainting, pour any remaining paint from the color cup back into the palette, or discard it.

FIG. 2. With a clean wet bristle brush, remove any pigment clinging to the inside of the cup; rinse the cup out; then spray clean water through the brush. Remove the needle and wipe it off with a clean rag. It may be left out of the brush or inserted part way until the brush is to be used again; otherwise the liquid remaining in the brush might dry around the needle, causing it to stick.

FIG. 3. If the needle does stick, loosen it gently with the pliers, rotating the needle as indicated by the arrow, so as to loosen the dried pigment; then remove the needle carefully by hand as is ordinarily done. Be careful not to bend the needle.

When paint will not come through the brush, it may be due to one of many reasons. First, loosen the handle of the brush and pull back on the finger lever to see if the needle is actually moving back as it should. If not, tighten the needle locknut.

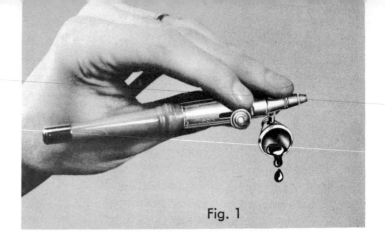

Fig. 1

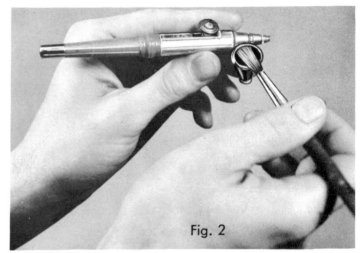

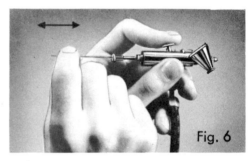

Fig. 2

Fig. 6

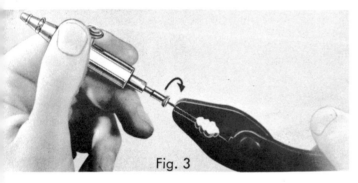

Fig. 3

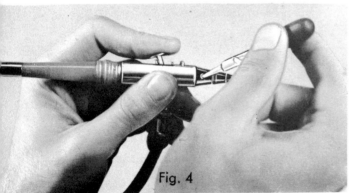

Fig. 4

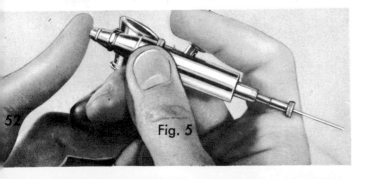

Fig. 5

FIG. 4. If the brush still does not function, remove the color cup. With the eye dropper, insert clean water directly into the airbrush, keeping the finger lever pulled back while squeezing water out of the eye dropper. If paint comes through the brush, it indicates that the cup is clogged, not the airbrush.

FIG. 5. Another method of unclogging the brush is to back up the paint by retracting the needle slightly, then pressing the forefinger over the air cap, while letting air through the brush. If this unclogs the brush, remove the cup and rinse it out thoroughly so that the pigment is not forced back into the brush again.

FIG. 6. Sometimes jiggling the needle back and forth gently will dislodge paint.

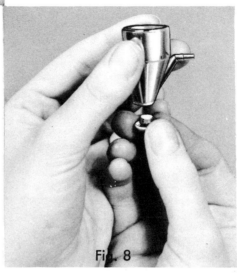

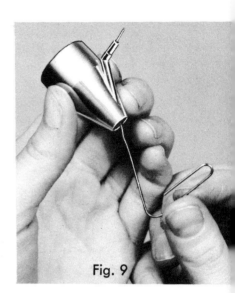

The Paasche Color Cup has a flat screw base on which it is possible to stand the cup upright when not in use. This is very practical, as one may use two or three different cups, each with different colors, when airpainting. In addition, this base can be unscrewed, exposing the color channel, so that cleaning or unclogging can be easily affected.

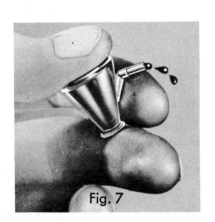

Fig. 7

Fig. 8

Fig. 9

FIG. 7. If the brush itself is clear, check the cup by filling it with water and pressing the thumb over the top, giving it a squeeze. The pressure should force the paint out of the opening unless the cup is very badly clogged. If it is [FIG. 8], remove the screw from the base and [FIG. 9] insert a flexible wire or a paper clip in the channel, pushing out the obstruction. Be certain to rescrew the base firmly as air might otherwise leak into the brush when operating, causing the brush to miss or sputter.

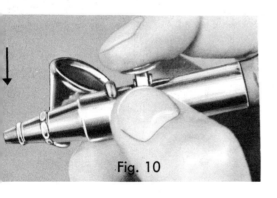

Fig. 10

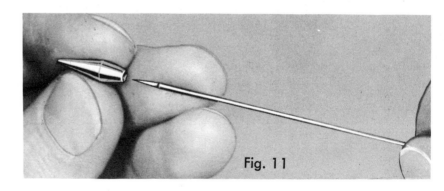

Fig. 11

FIG. 10. If, after having checked the needle and cup, the brush still does not function, check the air cap to see that it is properly screwed on, as this may be stopping the spray. If the difficulty still persists, remove the head of the brush and the tip.

FIG. 11. *Very gently* insert the reamer in the tip, revolve it, then pull it back. This will dislodge any foreign matter clogging the outlet. Do not use strong pressure with the reamer as it will spread open the tip and do more harm than good if abused. Blow air through the small end of the tip. Replace the tip in the brush, screw the head on firmly and try it again. If it still doesn't work, remove the valve nut and see if any dirt particles are in the valve spring. For anything else, try the repairman or factory.

Oiling Brush

FIG. 1. Oil should be used very sparingly and only in the two places indicated, where moving parts cause friction. A drop of machine oil or Vaseline may be applied with a match stick or wire to the back of the finger lever where it rubs against the rocker. The same may be done on the outside of the needle support, extending the support with the fingers as shown, while oiling, so that the oil will move back into the sleeve when released.

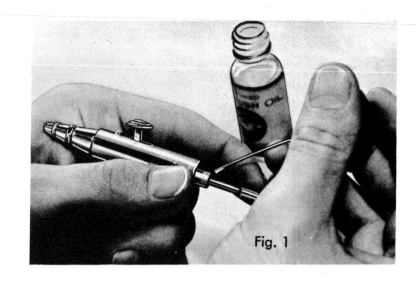

Fig. 1

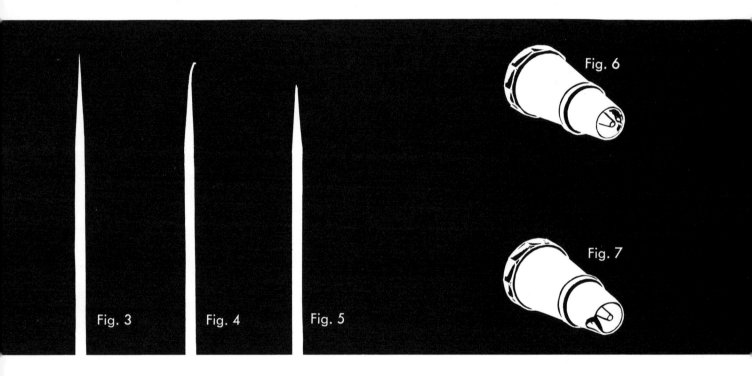

Fig. 3   Fig. 4   Fig. 5   Fig. 6   Fig. 7

FIG. 3. Airbrush needles are very fragile and should be handled with care. A good needle is straight and has a hairline point [FIG. 4]. A bent needle will cause the paint to spatter and may also split the airbrush tip if pulled out of the brush when in its bent condition. It is advisable to straighten it out with the thumb and forefinger before removing. If it is only slightly bent, it can be straightened by rotating it gently on an Arkansas stone [FIG. 5]. However, if the point is worn down very much the needle should be replaced with a new one as the fineness of the line drawn with the airbrush is partly dependent upon the sharpness of the needle [FIG. 6]. The air cap should be examined regularly as paint often dries on the inner surface. This may cause the paint to spatter or deflect the spray of paint. Clean the accumulated paint off by wetting and loosening it with a sable brush. A short blast of air will then help in cleaning it off [FIG. 7]. A dented air cap may also have this spattering effect.

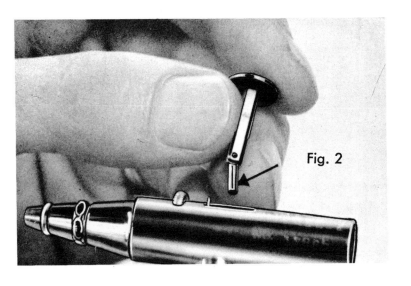

FIG. 2. A little Vaseline — not oil — should be placed also on the end of the lever piston to keep the valve lubricated. When taking the brush apart, it is advisable to clean the needle spring and leave a drop or two of oil on it.

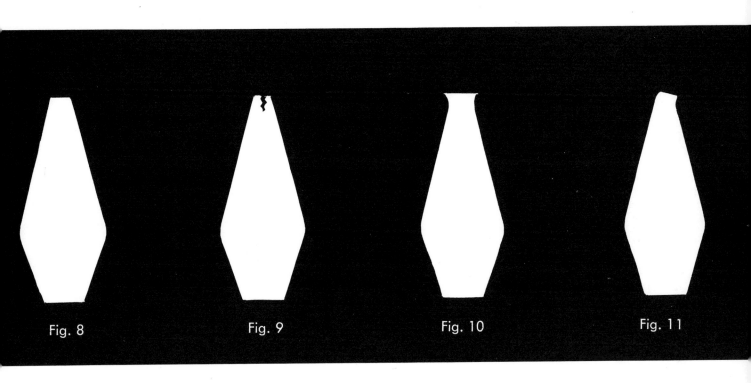

Fig. 8   Fig. 9   Fig. 10   Fig. 11

FIG. 8. The airbrush tip, shown here much larger than actual size, may be split by a bent needle or improper reaming [FIG. 9], or spread by pushing the needle into it too forcibly [FIG. 10], or deflected by being bumped against an object [FIG. 11]. The spread tip will cause the paint to spray out too abruptly when the finger lever is pulled back at the beginning of the stroke. It will also prevent a fine line from being made and may cause leaking of paint when the finger lever is pressed down only to release air. The other two tip injuries will cause spatter and deflections of the air pattern. The tip can be replaced as shown on page 150. If the old tip cannot be removed with the fingers pull it out with a pair of pliers as it cannot be repaired anyway. Be certain to screw the head on very tightly after replacing the tip.

Attaching Air Regulator to Carbon Dioxide (CO₂) Tank

The CO_2 tank will be delivered with the valve sealed. The upper projection, which is the gas outlet, is covered with a metal cap. Break off the wire seal, and remove the cap with a wrench, turning it counter-clockwise. The lower projection, a safety valve, should not be touched.

Unscrew the control valve *on the regulator* (counter-clockwise direction), so that air cannot pass through the regulator. It is important to do this before turning on the carbon dioxide valve as sudden pressure on the diaphragm would injure it. If the screw comes all the way out, merely replace it and screw in one or two turns.

Attach the regulator to the tank, screwing it in first by hand. Be certain that one or two washers have been inserted in the inlet of the regulator. Washers are supplied with the regulator. Be certain that the inlet cap is in a horizontal position so that the threads will not be stripped.

Open the valve of the *carbon dioxide tank* by turning the handle in a counter-clockwise direction. One or two turns should be sufficient.

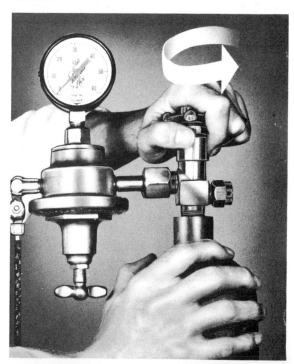

After hand tightening the inlet, complete the operation with a wrench. It should be as firm as possible.

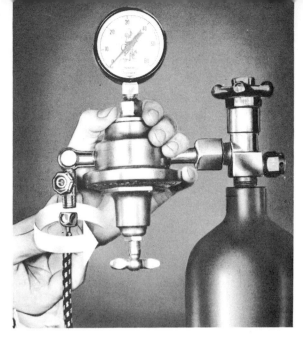

Screw the hose coupling to the valve of the regulator and tighten it firmly with the wrench. A small washer should be inserted in the hose coupling.

Now screw in the valve of the air regulator (clockwise direction), checking the air gauge until a pressure of about 30 pounds, less for fine work, is obtained.

Open up the outlet valve (counter-clockwise direction). Be certain to have the airbrush attached to the other end of this hose before opening up the valve, otherwise the carbon dioxide will escape. When turning off the air supply for the day, the valve on the tank itself should be closed firmly. For a temporary shut-off for changing brushes, etc., use the outlet valve.

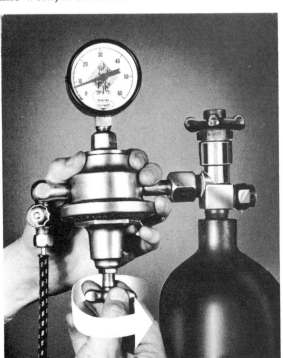

Index